VANISHED WATERS

A HISTORY OF SAN FRANCISCO'S MISSION BAY

NANCY OLMSTED

FOR

MISSION CREEK
CONSERVANCY

Copyright © 1986 Mission Creek Conservancy
300 Channel Street #21, San Francisco, California 94107
All rights reserved.
ISBN 0-9611492-1-3
Printed in the United States of America

Design: DuFlon Design Associates   Berkeley, California
Typography: Archetype   Berkeley, California
Printing: Edwards Brothers   Ann Arbor, Michigan

(Cover) *Scow schooner on Mission Bay.*
NAT'L MARITIME MUSEUM, S.F.

(Overleaf) *Fishing from Long Bridge in 1869. The yacht* Emerald,
winner of the San Francisco Yacht Club's first regatta,
is moored alongside. Stereo view by Edweard Muybridge.
BANCROFT LIBRARY

Office of the Mayor
SAN FRANCISCO

DIANNE FEINSTEIN

August 22, 1986

To the Friends of the Mission Creek Conservancy

San Franciscans have always had a great pride of place. The rich history of the City, its vibrant economy, the unique architecture, and its fine weather all combine to make living here deeply pleasurable. Individual neighborhoods, each with its own character and community, the bustling Financial District, and an unsurpassed retailing district near Union Square form the principal patterns of the City's beautiful tapestry. We cherish our town because it is so livable. The commitment of San Franciscans to preserving its human scale helps create that livability.

Mission Bay, now an area of underused industrial buildings and railroad tracks, will become one of the great neighborhoods of San Francisco. As a friend of the Mission Creek Conservancy I am sure you share a deep concern for the livability of the City's new community, as do I. In this book the Conservancy is making us aware of the shorebirds and boats on Mission Creek, of the Creek itself and its history. They ask us to respect these touchstones to an earlier time, these natural and colorful qualities, and to provide for them appropriately in developing a bright new design for Mission Bay.

As we plan for the pattern of housing, jobs and public places that will comprise this new addition to San Francisco, the Conservancy has engaged the noted local historian, Nancy Leigh Olmsted, to write this informative and lively guide to the history of Mission Bay and its surroundings.

We are grateful for these expressions of concern and for this information about Mission Bay.

Warm personal regards.

Sincerely yours,

Dianne Feinstein
Mayor

DF:CF

DEDICATION

We will ever strive for the ideals
 and sacred things of the city,
 both alone and with many.

We will seek unceasingly to quicken
 the sense of public duty.

We will transmit this city
 not only not less,
 but greater, better,
 and more beautiful
 than it was transmitted to us.

                    —*oath of the Athenian city-state*

PREFACE

The Mission Creek Conservancy is a public benefit corporation dedicated to preserving and enhancing the tidal community on Mission Creek in San Francisco. This special place deserves to be respected in the massive changes proposed by Santa Fe Pacific Realty Company for its Mission Bay development.

The Mission Bay project, encompassing some 300 acres in all, will occupy an area that, until just 150 years ago was a salt marsh, abounding with marine life, shorebirds and wild mammals. Even now the channel hosts great egrets, great blue herons, cormorants and grebes. The Mission Creek Conservancy sees an opportunity and a mandate in this new Mission Bay development to create a shoreline park and wildlife habitat unique in San Francisco.

With the generous help of the San Francisco Foundation, the Mission Creek Conservancy commissioned and published *Vanished Waters* to acquaint San Franciscans with the fascinating history of this part of the City, and to thereby foster their respect for the place. This book tells about the geological changes that formed Mission Bay; its banks teeming with life that lay as a banquet table for the estuary's shorebirds; the Coast Indians who lived here in harmony with nature for more than 5,000 years; and mostly about the immigrants who, in just 150 years have filled Mission Bay, parcelled it, sold and resold it, built boats and run saloons on it, and have otherwise brought it to this end of the 20th Century, where it awaits our turning it to yet another set of uses.

We have the ability to preserve the historic character that remains in the boats, the bridges and the shorebirds. We can satisfy the demands of our growing City without paving over this remnant of a wetland community that can still enrich our lives in important ways.

Nancy Leigh Olmsted brings a fortunate combination of talents to this work. She is not only a historian, steeped in the history of San Francisco's waterfront and fascinated by the people who shaped it. She is also a guide who conducts walking tours of the waterfront. Thus, *Vanished Waters* takes on the double aspect of a history, enlivened by words and works of the people who lived it, and of a guided walk through the places that were and are here. Join us on Mrs. Olmsted's informative and engaging tour of Mission Bay and its surroundings.

(Above) Birdseye View of Southern San Francisco, ca. 1876 . . .
George Goddard drew this remarkable aerial perspective of Mission
Bay looking across Ocean Beach toward Long Bridge that spanned the
bay from a line of Fourth Street south to the Potrero and on to
Hunters Point. Mission Creek drainage is in the upper center, Islais
Creek on the upper right.

INTRODUCTION

The history of Mission Bay is the story of the gradual filling-in of a vast tidal cove in San Francisco Bay. Covered with shallow waters of Mission Bay, edged with tidal salt-marshes and receiving fresh water from meandering Mission Creek, this broad, sunny expanse of real-estate has over the last 130 years attracted a wide variety of would-be settlers, imaginative speculators, and visionary planners.

First the salt marshes, mudflats and estuaries were bridged over, then filled in with the city's unwanted sandhills. Finally, as it was planked and paved, the fill extended farther and farther—eventually reaching out into greater San Francisco Bay to engulf Mission Rock. This slow process adapted to changing technologies: planked toll-roads for the horse-and-buggy; Long Bridge, a causeway with rails, for the horsecar; a ferry landing for railroad freight cars from Oakland; a broad network of tracks, a roundhouse and freight warehouses for the railroad; and now, high arcs of concrete freeways designed to carry automobiles and trucks above the ground.

To understand how these physical changes happened, it is necessary to untangle a cat's cradle of promises, court decisions, legislative actions, planners' visions and speculators' schemes—some so frankly fraudulent that newspaper articles, now yellow with age, sputtered in outraged protest. All of this was part and parcel of the charged-up history of San Francisco. The land that was California, after centuries of natural evolution, was literally turned upside down and inside out in the hunt for gold, all within a decade. Speculation was so feverish in this over-heated population that it spread from gambling tables to real estate, and deeds for the city's water lots were swapped and sold as if they were cards played on green felt cloth.

The story of Mission Bay moves back and forth from the changing physical reality of the land—best understood from maps and photographs—to the less easily comprehended doings of such a self-acknowledged rogue as Asbury Harpending, of the self-appointed "Judge" John McHenry and the eccentric William Cornell Jewett, and of the "infamous" Dr. Peter Smith, who went to court to collect what was due him from the city. In so doing, he set off such a scandal of land speculation that the city fathers stood accused of "giving away the city's patrimony."

The history of Mission Bay, long concealed, is even now only half revealed. Information from deed books of the 1850s yields new evidence of the impressive scope of Gold Rush wheeling and dealing. It also introduces new dramatis personae who must become subjects of another book. An old letter from Jasper O'Farrell, the city surveyor, takes on new significance, but opens questions requiring research beyond the scope of this modest work. Each person interviewed knew of someone else "not to be missed." But time and pages come to an end, so the hidden history of Mission Bay raises some tantalizing speculations for both reader and author, and that is the fascination of history.

Scow Schooner Days on Channel Creek. . . *In 1906 my Uncle Bill worked for a while at E. K. Wood Lumberyard on Channel Creek. He recalls the scow schooners coming and going and the thirst of many of their crews. When they reached the creek, they sometimes made a careless mooring in their haste to get up to the "Old Corner" and hoist a few steams. Occasionally, when the tide turned, a scow would come drifting down on the Third Street drawbridge with no one aboard. Consternation and shouting from the bridge tender might turn up someone to lasso her before she got jammed in the works. Uncle Bill says that if you shouted "Captain!" on the hay wharves or in the nearby saloons, every other man would turn his head.* Karl Kortum, Chief Curator National Maritime Museum, San Francisco

CONTENTS

WATER ON THE LAND—
THE COAST PEOPLE

About 15,000 years ago the level of the sea began to rise, and over the next 10,000 years ocean waters gradually drowned the great inland valley of an ancient river that had carved the deep canyon of the Golden Gate with the sands of the Sierra, carried in snowmelt to the sea. The ancient river canyon was cut 15,000 to 20,000 years ago when the sea was more than 300 feet below its present level and the coastline was the far side of the Farallon Islands.[3] The ocean did not spill through the Golden Gate all at once with a great shaking of the earth, as the Indians recounted, but filled in slowly as the great glaciers of the last ice age melted, raising the sea level. Filling first the deepest canyons of the great river, the sea rose until it reached a point 381 feet above the river's bedrock at the Golden Gate.

The tidal lagoon of Mission Bay was created late in this 25,000-year period of rising sea, which reached its present height about 5,000 years ago. A contoured underwater ridge, 200 feet above the floor of the bay, extends south from Rincon Hill (near the western footing of the San Francisco Bay Bridge) to Mission Rock at the outer edge of Mission Bay. It then curves northeast to include Yerba Buena Island, channeling water to the east.[4]

This relatively recent event was not the first time the ocean flooded the floor of the bay—the presence of seawater has been traced back 125,000 years. Beneath the layers of mud and peat sediments that underlie Mission Bay there may be another far more ancient alluvium floor. After the last ice-melt raised the ocean level, Mission Bay extended over at least 560 acres of tidal mudflat. By the time of the Coast Survey Map of 1852, the silt deposited by the tides had transformed the 300 acres above normal high-water into salt marsh, leaving 260 acres of shallow lagoon covered by a foot or more of water at low tide.

The 260 acres of shallow seawater spread out to receive the sun like a great floating greenhouse. As microscopic diatoms, eel grass and other plant life photosynthesized the sun's energy, generations of underwater vegetation grew superabundant grazing grounds for such herbivores as sea snails. Unconsumed plants decayed into the mud, feeding microscopic bacteria. If not swept out by the tides, the residues formed layers of peat on the bottom. Twice a day seawater swept in waves of tiny crustaceans to nourish the millions of mussels and other filter feeders that burrowed in the rich ooze, awaiting the tidal surge.

The incoming tides carried sediments from the engulfed river and the ocean. Mud and sand built up along the edges of the lagoon, forming islands that sprouted cordgrass and, at the higher levels, pickleweed. The lagoon began evolving into a salt marsh, the most energy-productive source of life of all natural habitats. As salt marshes do, it gave more to the world's ecosystem than it received.[5]

Except for the occasional winter storm, blowing in from the southeast, Mission Bay remained a lagoon and marshland of calm, protected sunny water. With such a setting it became the banquet ground for an enormous bird population, both the year-round residents, such as the phenomenal duck community, and the migrating birds, among them the Canadian geese and visiting loons. "The smelt turned the water silver," attracting egrets, herons, osprey and gulls.[6] Hawks, owls and falcons fed on multitudes of mice, shrews and rabbits in the upper reaches of the salt marsh.

The variety of the landscape at Mission Bay added to the abundance and diversity of plant and animal life, as a winding, fresh-water stream joined the salt marsh from the west. One of many small streams that originated in Twin

Peaks, Mission Creek first appeared as a small waterfall that fed a pond fringed with willows and then made its way into the tidal estuary of Mission Bay. (Within historic times the site of the pond underlay what is now Seventeenth to Nineteenth streets at Valencia; Mission Creek joined the tidal arm of Mission Bay at Sixteenth Street).[7]

The Coming of the Coast People—Into this landscape that was more water than dry land, the coast people came, skimming over the shallow water of Mission Bay in their balsas, the bouyant watercraft made of tule reeds lashed together in bundles. With pointed sticks they pried mussels from rocks and dug up clams; with woven baskets they scooped up smelt; with throwing nets weighted by grooved stones, they snared ducks and shorebirds. Independent of the tides, they could paddle up Mission Creek to cut willow withes for their baskets and for lashings to hold the pole framework of their huts. In the brackish back-water along the creek, they harvested the tule reeds that gave them new boats, fibers for their sleeping mats and aprons, and thatch for their conical houses. Beside fresh-water springs they set up their encampments, living lightly on the land until the season changed or their food supply was exhausted and they had to move on within their tribal territory.

It is uncertain when the wandering coast people first appeared on Mission Bay. Burial mounds with artifacts and middens dating back to an estimated 3,500 BC were found on Hunters Point, some near the shore at Candlestick Park.[8] The people of these mounds may have been the ancestors of the Costanoans, as the Spanish named the coast people. The Costanoan linguistic group, comprised of eight separate languages spoken by 50 autonomous tribes (each with its own dialect), has been traced to 500 A.D. At the time the Spanish arrived the coast people had fished the waters of Mission Bay for 1,275 years. They numbered

Earliest European view of the Coast People. *Unique among California Indians, the double-bladed paddle was a special innovation of the coast people. With its pointed prow the buoyant balsa could carry four people, swiftly and easily, into inlets and coves, from island to island in the bay. The Spanish invention in this view is the woven, striped blanket, made by the women neophytes at the mission. This is the earliest view we have of the coast people, made in 1816 by Louis Choris, a world traveler of acute perception who wrote, "I have never seen one laugh. I have never seen one look one in the face. They look as though they are interested in nothing." By 1816, this was true.*[14]

THREE

Bowstrings were made of sinew or vegetable fibers. *Arrows were tipped with chipped stone or bone arrowheads and the shanks had feathers attached with asphaltum. Quivers for the arrows appear to be fox skins in this view. These San Francisco Bay Indians are not drawn as a European would have imagined them to be, but are close representations. On this same voyage, Choris made careful drawings of Pacific islanders and Eskimos. His detailed renderings of their artifacts are so correct from an anthropological viewpoint that we can have confidence that his watercolors and lithographs of the coast people are equally accurate.*

10,000, all in the same linguistic group, of which 1,400 are thought to have spoken *Ramaytush*—the language spoken by the group most closely associated with Mission Bay.[9]

The Coast People, Half Revealed—We do not know the name they called themselves. "Costanoan" has been the useful descriptive category for the people who belonged to this large linguistic group and lived on San Francisco Peninsula as far south as Monterey on the ocean side. Indians living in the Bay Area today reject "Costanoan" because it is Spanish; they prefer "Ohlone," meaning "the abalone people," which is closer to their own conception of their ancestors' identity.[10] Studies of basket fragments and materials found in middens, descriptions of the tribes' physical and social life set down by the Spanish Fathers and visiting explorers (mostly in the early 19th century), plus the threads of memory recorded in ethnographers' field notes of the early 20th century—these form the basis for all later accounts of the coast people. The fundamental agreement of these sources, as late as many of them are, is the basis for what follows.

The Coast People on Mission Bay—That the coast people had an encampment at Mission Bay seems certain. The small lake edged with willows, and Mission Creek leading directly to the sheltered feeding ground for thousands of birds, made the sunny bay the perfect setting for a people whose choice of food was mussels. Whether their settlement was large or small, temporary or permanent, we cannot say.

Tribelets ranged from 50 to 500 members; the average village had about 200 people. Larger groups were more likely to have a permanent central village with outlying, temporary camps placed near specific food sources. The absence of oaks at Mission Bay, in a culture where acorns were used every day as a staple food in the form of gruel or small cakes, suggests that Mission Bay was one of several temporary encampments visited periodically from a permanent village further inland.

One of the puzzles about California Indians is the fact that the languages of the tribes differed so greatly, even within the same linguistic group. Captain Juan Bautista de Anza, for example, brought an Indian from Monterey to San Francisco to serve as interpreter, but even though he was a Costanoan he could not understand Indians in the Bay Area. Anza also discovered that his Indian guides were afraid to cross specific physical boundaries; a certain territory was allotted to each tribe, and boundaries were respected.

Whatever the reasons for this multiplicity of small, isolated tribes, one result was to spread the Indian population out over the land. Food supplies were not over-used, so each tribe could count on having enough roots, berries, seeds and acorns. The Indians developed a sophisticated method for making sure crops of clover and other annuals were abundant; they set fire to certain grasslands every year, which assured them of a fast second crop with plenty of seeds and bounteous grazing for the deer they hunted. But beyond this practice they planted no crops; they depended instead on the natural course of the seasons to bring them berries, acorns, amole plant, wild onions and the roots of lilies. One indication of the coast people's self-sufficiency is that although they supplied inland Yokut Indians with salt, mussels, abalone shells and dried abalone meat, their only import was pinon pine nuts. So abundant was the wildlife near Mission Bay that quail could be killed by throwing stones, rabbits caught by hand and fish scooped up by the basketful.

Baskets for gathering, cooking and storage were essential to the coast people's existence. The bracken fern, sedges, rushes, tule and willow were woven into a wide variety of shapes and sizes. They decorated these twined baskets with olivella-shell beads, quail feathers, abalone pendants and woodpecker crests of red feathers. Not only did they decorate their baskets, they painted themselves with hematite, cinnabar and white clay, and wore necklaces of shell beads.[12]

The coast people played music on flutes fashioned from hollowed alder branches, whistles made from hollow bird bones and rattles made with cocoons. They decorated their bodies for the dances and music that were their ceremonial celebrations. Their dances went on for hours. Sometimes just the men danced, other dances were performed by the medicine men, still others were reserved for women. Among their traditional dances were the coyote dance, the dove dance and the bear dance. Dancing sometimes seemed to produce a state of self-hypnosis in which the coast people were seen to swallow live embers.[13]

The religion of the tribes was a mixture of witchcraft and their belief in magic, myths and the importance of their dreams. All of this would have made them particularly vulnerable to the Spanish missionaries. Mission music and ritual chanting at high mass had great fascination for the neophytes. The importance their own ceremonies had for the Indians was matched by the great significance religion held for the Spanish Fathers.

THE SPANISH PRESENCE AT MISSION BAY, 1775-1833

The first European boat to explore the waters of Mission Bay was a *cayuco*, or dugout, made from the trunk of a redwood taken from the bank of the Carmel River and brought into San Francisco Bay on August 2, 1775, aboard the *San Carlos*. As the *San Carlos* lay anchored off Angel Island, pilot Juan Bautista Aquirre followed his instructions to explore the southeastern part of San Francisco Bay. No diary has survived, but all later accounts agree that as the Spanish pilot entered Mission Bay he saw three Indians on shore, and they were weeping. He named the protected bay *Ensenada de los Llorones*—or Cove of the Weepers.[15] Thus Mission Bay was discovered by the Spanish and given a name that seems prophetic for its native inhabitants.

More accustomed to horses than to boats, the Spanish soldiers and Franciscan padres explored the land around San Francisco Bay from 1769 to 1776. Considerably confused, they tried to determine if the watery expanses they saw from the hills and shores were rivers flowing into the bay or land-locked arms of the bay itself. They were charged with finding the best sites for a fort and two missions that would establish the church north of Monterey.

Using an astrolabe and a compass borrowed from the Carmel Mission, Father Pedro Font drew the best map to survive these expeditions and keyed it to his diary descriptions, complete with pen sketches of the islands in the bay. On March 29, 1776, enroute from the site chosen for the future presidio to find the most suitable spot for a mission nearby, he wrote: "Although in all my travels I saw very good sites and beautiful country, I saw none which pleased me as much as this. And I think it could be well-settled, like Europe, there would not be anything more beautiful. . . . Passing through wooded hills and over flats with good lands we encountered two lagoons and some springs of good water with plentiful grass, fennel and other useful herbs, we arrived at a beautiful arroyo which, because it was Friday of the Sorrows, we called *Arroyo de los Dolores*. On its banks we found much and very fragrant manzanita and other plants and wild violets. It [Mission Creek] enters the plain by a fall which it makes on emerging from the hills, and with it all can be irrigated, and at the same fall a mill can be erected, for it is very suitable to that purpose. Near the arroyo Moraga planted a little maize and chick peas to test the soil, which appeared very good and I concluded that this place was very pretty and the best for the establishment of one of the two missions." (The Santa Clara Mission was founded three months later.)[16]

In June of that same year, a number of Captain Anza's original settlers from Sonora, now under the leadership of Lt. Jose Joaquin Moraga and Fathers Francis Palou and Pedro Benito Cambon, set out from Monterey to San Francisco. It took ten days with many stops for the struggling procession to make the trip. Some twenty soldiers, seven settlers and their families (including pregnant women and very small children), five vaqueros and muleteers to ride herd on 200 head of cattle, and a mule train carrying maize and beans finally arrived at the small freshwater lagoon at the head of Mission Creek. This headwater lake they named *Nuestra Senora de los Dolores*, and it was here that they pitched their fifteen tents, as Father Palou praised God that they had arrived unharmed at the site for the Mission of San Francisco de Asis. He noted in his journal that the Indians were astonished at the sight of cattle and mules, and brought mussels and wild seeds as gifts, curious to see the first white women and children to arrive at Mission Bay.

For a month the little group of settlers waited for the *San Carlos*, which was

Indian Neophyte. *Sketched by Louis Choris' sympathetic hand, this native Californian's expressive face speaks to us with eloquence of the suffering of her people.*

BANCROFT LIBRARY

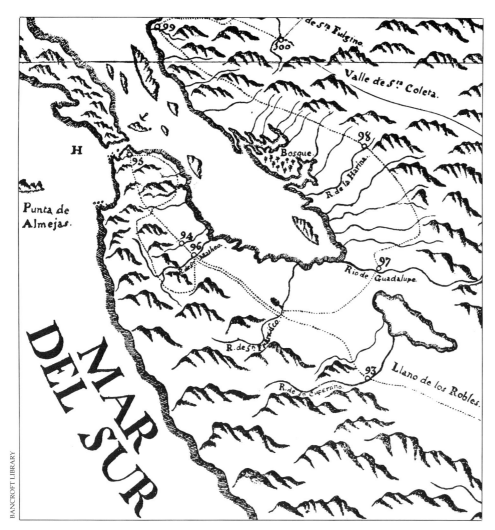

Father Pedro Font's map of San Francisco Bay. *Made in 1777, it shows the route taken by various Spanish expeditions around the bay. Figure 95 is keyed to his diary description of the presidio site.*
The trail south, which follows the shore of the bay until it cuts inland south of Yerba Buena Island, led them to Mission Creek and the site of the Mission San Francisco de Asis. Figure 96 locates San Mateo and 97 is the site of Mission Santa Clara on Rio de Guadalupe, the second mission, founded three months after the one at San Francisco.

to bring carpenters and tools from Monterey; meanwhile Lt. Moraga explored the hills, discovering many springs of fresh water and several small lakes. When after some time the *San Carlos* had not arrived, he put his men to work building the presidio, leaving Fathers Palou and Cambon at the mission site with six soldiers, a settler and the cattle. When the *San Carlos* finally arrived, they learned that she had been blown off course all the way to San Diego, then sailed as far north as Point Reyes, missing the Golden Gate. When she did make her way into San Francisco Bay, work proceeded on building the Mission of San Francisco de Asis. The presidio was dedicated on September 17 and the mission on October 9, both with all the fanfare, firepower and ceremony the Spanish could muster.

In Palou's diary he noted that the Indians were so frightened at the sound of the ceremonial cannon firing that they fled the scene. He seems to have contradicted himself, for in an August 12 entry he recorded that the Salsonas (southern Indians from the rancheria near San Mateo) had defeated the local Indians in a great fight, burning their huts so that they were forced to flee on their rafts. For several months after the battle no Indians came to hunt ducks on Mission Bay or trade with the Spanish for beads and food. The Mission San Francisco de Assisi at Dolores was completed and there were no Indians to be converted, nor did any appear until the following spring.[17]

The Indians as Perceived—From their diaries and letters we know that the Spanish fathers viewed the California Indians as lost children, incapable of understanding beyond a simple level. Further, they saw them as lost souls, doomed to eternal suffering unless converted and baptized. The priests were appalled at the nearly naked Indians, smeared with mud to keep out the cold, living on acorn mush, in huts made of reeds. They saw themselves as inspired rescuers. Their plan was to clothe the Indians and teach them to weave cloth;

to improve their diet and teach them to raise beans, corn, and fruit; to build permanent houses and teach them to make adobe bricks. This plan would take about ten years, the padres calculated, then the Christian Indians would settle their families on small farms, effectively colonizing California. The saving of their souls would proceed at the same time.

Fear and fascination were the means for saving souls. The adobe walls of the mission were painted with the glories of heaven emblazoned above, and below, fiery scenes of explicit tortures reserved for the damned. The recruited neophytes were quick to learn the Lord's Prayer in Spanish and to follow the rituals of the mass. In return they were free to roam within the confines of the mission, where they attended services and found the music of bells, flutes and a small violin captivating. Missionary zeal can best be understood as the padres' conception of an inspired rescue effort: overcome all obstacles and save the Indians from the observed hardships of this world and the certain tortures of the next.

Trouble at the San Francisco Mission—After the death of Father Serra in August 1784, followed by the departure of Father Palou for Mexico, life for the Indian converts at Mission Bay became more and more repressive. Diego de Borica, one of the most enlightened governors of California, began to look into complaints from Father J.M. Fernandez. After sleepless nights and much worry, he had written that in 1795, 203 Indians died and 200 escaped at San Francisco. The Indians were compelled to do excessive work, handcuffed, imprisoned and beaten for the most trivial offences. "When the miserable Indians, learning too late that their former gentile life, even with its precariousness, was far preferable to Christianization . . . they attempted to regain their freedom by flight. They were hunted down and punished with tenfold vigor."[18]

Borica intervened at once, putting some reforms into effect, but still the Indians left the San Francisco mission at every opportunity. It is from the accounts of a handful of visitors, perhaps ten in all, that we know how the Spanish tried and failed. It should be remembered that these observers of San Francisco's mission, much as they deplored the means and effect of religious conversion, looked upon the California Indians in their natural state as uncivilized and in need of help. Accounts written after 1815 began to list the grim statistics of Indian death by disease: measles, cholera, smallpox and "the disease given them by the Spanish soldiers" or syphilis.

Otto von Kotzebue's Account, 1816—". . . We entered the church . . . where we found some hundreds of half-naked Indians upon their knees, who although they neither understood Spanish nor Latin, are not allowed to miss one mass after their conversion. As the missionaries on their side, do not endeavour to learn the language of the natives, I cannot conceive in what manner they have been taught the Christian religion; the confusion in the heads and hearts of these poor people, who only know how to mimic external ceremonies must be very great . . . we were shown the dwelling-places of the Indians, consisting of long, low, clay-built houses, forming several streets. The filthy state of these barracks was beyond conception, which is probably the cause of the great mortality among the inhabitants, since of the 1000 Indians in San Francisco, 300 die annually. . . . Twice a year they are permitted to go home, which short time for them is the happiest; and I have sometimes seen them going, in large numbers, shouting on the road. The sick, who cannot undertake the journey, accompany their fortunate countrymen to the shore, where they embark, and remain sitting for days together, casting their sorrowful eyes on the distant hills . . . probably they would flee away altogether, were it not for fear of the soldiers, who take them, and bring them back like criminals . . . this fear is so great that seven or eight dragoons are enough to keep in check hundreds of Indians."[19]

Captain Frederick William Beechey's Narrative, 1826—"If any captured Indians show a repugnance to conversion it is the practice to imprison them for

a few days, and then allow them to breathe a little fresh air in a walk around the mission to observe the happy life of their converted countrymen; after which they are shut up, and thus continue to be incarcerated until they declare their readiness to renounce the religion of their forefathers . . . the Indians are so averse to confinement that they very soon become impressed with the manifestly superior and more comfortable mode of life of those who are at liberty. . . . Having become Christians they are put to trades, or if they have good voices are taught music . . . there are weavers, tanners, shoemakers, bricklayers, carpenters, blacksmiths . . . others are taught to rear cattle and horses, some to cook for the Mission; while the females card, clean and spin wool, weave and sew. In requital of these benefits the services of the Indians belong to the Mission for life, and if any neophyte should repent . . . and desert, an armed force is sent in pursuit and drags him back to punishment. . . . The animosity between wild and converted Indians is of great importance to the missions as it checks desertions. . . . The Mission in San Francisco contained a thousand converts in 1817, who were housed in small huts around the Mission; but at present [1826] only 260 remain. . . . The huts of the absentees had all fallen into decay, and presented heaps of filth and rubbish; while the remaining inmates of the mission were in miserable condition."[20]

The Failure of the Missions Becomes Evident to All—In Mexico a revolution broke out in 1810 that was anti-clerical, with the result that the annual stipend of $400 was not paid to the Franciscans from 1811 to 1818. Government ships no longer stopped on any regular basis to pick up exports and drop off supplies. The Mexican agitation resulted in the secularization of all the mission lands in 1833. By then, only 204 converted Indians were left at Mission Bay.[21]

It Seemed Their Dancing Never Stopped. *"In their dances the Indians remain almost always in the same place, endeavoring, partly with their bows and arrows, partly with the feathers they hold in their hands and wear on their heads, and also by measured springs, by different movements of their bodies, and by facial contortions, to imitate scenes of battle or of domestic life. Their music consists of singing and clapping with a stick at one end. The women have their own particular song, and their own particular way of dancing. They hop about near the men, but never in time with them. Their principal action is in pressing the abdomen with the thumb and forefinger, first to one side and then to the other. . . ." So wrote G.H. von Landsdorff, the German doctor who accompanied Nicolai Rezanov on the Russian expedition to northern California on the* Juno *in 1806.*[22]

RANCHO LIFE, 1833-1846

In a measure designed to reduce the power of the church and open the rich mission lands to colonization, the Mexican Congress passed a secularization bill in August 1833. Advocates of the law could point out that more than fifty years of the friars' teaching—the inculcation of Christian civilization and the rudiments of agriculture and industry—could be considered adequate to prepare the Indian converts for self sufficiency. At each of California's twenty-one missions, an administrator "would give to every adult male Indian a tract of twenty-eight acres; his fair share of one half of the domestic animals and tools of the Mission."[23] The appearance of liberality, however, only thinly concealed the wholesale looting of mission property, as the departing friars and newly appointed administrators strove to prevent each other from self-enrichment by appropriating what they could. Between the announcement of the new policy and the appointment of the local administrator, the 5,000 cattle at Mission San Francisco de Asis were driven away, while the few remaining Indians simply walked away.

The secularization of the missions set off a wave of Mexican land grants in California under a process that dated back to an 1824 law, the Law of Colonialization. The procedure was a simple one in which the petitioner asked the governor of Mexico for a specific tract of empty land. This written request was frequently accompanied by a *diseño*, or map, prepared locally by a rough ground survey. If the petitioner had performed some service for the government, such as being part of the army, the claim was generally granted. Since the act aimed to encourage settlement, land grants were made to petitioners of foreign origin as well, provided they formally adopted both the Catholic faith and Mexican citizenship; many of these petitioners married the daughters of Mexican families.

The 1824 law set a legal maximum of 48,400 acres, and the average ranch was about 22,000 acres. If the land was irrigated by fresh water, no one person was allowed more than 4,400 acres—as was the case with Bernal's Rancho at Islais Creek and Hunters Point. Under the original law of 1824, lands owned by the mission were not subject to petition, but with the 1833 secularization act much of California's most valuable land was free to be awarded to colonists. They had only to qualify and agree to fence the land, erect permanent dwellings, and protect the rights of previous inhabitants (that is, the Indians), who became free labor for the rancho owners. From 1834 through 1845, 95 percent of the great California ranchos were created.[24]

The Bernal and de Haro Families, Gente de Razon—Two families laid claim to most of the land of the Potrero—the Bernals and the de Haros. Potrero translates from Spanish to "pasture." San Francisco had two potreros: The Bernals claimed the *potrero viejo* (old grazing lands that extended from Islais Creek south to Hunters Point) and the de Haros claimed the *potrero nuevo* (new pasturelands appropriated from the mission and around Mission Bay to Potrero Point).

Both the Bernals and the de Haros were *gente de razon*, or people of reason (in contrast to the Indians, believed to be without reason). By 1840, H.H. Bancroft estimates, there were no more than 800 *gente de razon* at San Francisco, Sonoma and the Peninsula. Large families with twelve to fifteen children were usual, a fact that some foreign observers attributed to the miracle of California's fecund climate. In less than a generation most of the *gente de razon* were related.[25]

Accounts of rancho life written during this period generally agree on the simplicity of rural Mexican-Californian life. A typical passage by Walter Colton, *alcalde* of Monterey from 1846 to 1849: "There are no people I have ever been among who enjoy life so thoroughly as the Californians. Their habits are simple; their wants are few; nature rolls almost everything spontaneously into their lap.

The bear hunt.
"The king of all sports in California is the bear-hunt . . . Each rider now uncoiled his lasso from its loggerhead and held it ready to spring from his hand, like a hooped serpent from the brake. The bear . . . plunged from the thicket . . . and was leaping, with giant bounds . . . for the dark covert of the forest beyond . . . one looped him around the neck and brought him to a momentary stand. As soon as bruin felt the lasso, he growled his defiant thunder and sprung in rage at the horse. . . . The horse knew as well as his rider, that the safety of both depended on his keeping the lasso taut. . . ." From the journal of Walter Colton, a navy chaplain who became alcalde *of Monterey in 1846.*[33]
AUTHOR'S COLLECTION

Their hospitality knows no bounds . . . always glad to see you, they only regret that your business calls you away."[26]

But all was not so peaceful as most accounts would have us believe. John Vioget's tavern, the only public house in Yerba Buena village in the 1840s, became the center for drunken brawls between Mexican-Californians and outsiders. José C. Bernal was called up several times in two years for drunken fights and knife stabbings. The de Haro twins were sentenced to serve six months in jail in San Jose for wounding Captain Elliot Libbey, master of the bark *Tasso*, who had made advances to a young lady much beloved by "Chico" de Haro. These incidents (recorded by the *juez de paz*) demonstrated that Mexican-Californians were not able to accept with equanimity the idea that Yankees appeared to be in California to stay, to marry their daughters and settle on their land.

Both José C. Bernal and Francisco de Haro served the Mexican government in the army. Bernal was a soldier at the presidio, born of a soldier, Juan Bernal, who had accompanied Anza to Monterey in 1776. Both father and son were stationed at the presidio and both kept cattle and sheep as a second occupation. Bernal's first petition to the *Rincon Salinas y Potrero Viejo* ("the corner of the salt marsh and the old grazing lands") was rejected on grounds that the land was common grazing land, but he persisted and his claim was confirmed in 1840.

Francisco de Haro was a relatively educated man in a society where few could read or sign their names. He had served as personal secretary to Governor Arguello, was *alcalde* of Yerba Buena in 1834 and again in 1838-39 when he assisted Vioget in surveying the village. De Haro's twin sons, Ramon and Francisco, were "empowered to occupy provisionally the piece of land called *Potrero de San Francisco* to the extent of half a square league" (2,288 acres of land near the mission and Mission Bay).[28]

But an ugly incident was to mark the end of an era. Occupation by the de Haro boys was to be very short; born in 1827, they died in 1846 at the moment their country became part of the United States. It was at the time that John C. Fremont, accompanied by Kit Carson and a band of Americans, determined to seize Sonoma as his part in the United States' takeover of California. In retribution for an earlier murder of two Americans, the twin boys were shot, along with their uncle, Antonio Berreyesa. The news of the twins' death came as a great shock to Francisco de Haro, who died on New Year's Day, 1849; his death attributed to his grief.[29]

More Promises on the Land . . . Commodore Sloat, July 7, 1847—After raising the American flag at the Customs House in Monterey on the morning of July 7, 1848, Commodore John Sloat promised the assembled Mexican-Californian population, "All peoples holding titles to real-estate, or in quiet possession of lands under color of right, should have their titles and rights guaranteed to them." By July 11, acting under Sloat's orders to Commander John B. Montgomery, the American flag flew over San Francisco and, to the north, over Sonoma and Bodega. American possession of California was a fact, and Sloat's promise to the Mexican-Californians lay on the future of the land.

Kearny Sets a Precedent—Meanwhile the government in Washington had directed General Stephen W. Kearny to establish a temporary civil government with himself as provisional military governor. The limits of Kearny's authority were at once sweeping and vague; his charge was to maintain order.

The general stretched that authority when, on March 10, 1847, he proceeded to "grant, convey and release to the town of San Francisco, all title of the U.S. in beach and water lots between Fort Montgomery and Rincon Point . . . The lots released were to be sold at auction for the benefit of the town.[31] The concept established by Kearny's action shaped the future of South Beach and Mission Bay: California real-estate under water could be auctioned to keep San Francisco financially afloat and water lots were investments in the future.[32]

Vaqueros lassoing cattle.
"All of the cattle were branded, and each rancho had ear-marks . . . Owners of adjoining ranchos came to the rodeo grounds to select their own cattle and brought with them their own vaqueros who went in and picked out the cattle belonging to their special ranchos. The work of separating the cattle, while a necessity, was really more of an amusement than a labor . . . it was an opportunity to exchange greetings and talk over affairs." William Heath Davis, Sixty Years in California, 1831 to 1889.
AUTHORS COLLECTION

THE GOLDEN ERA, 1848-1853

At the height of the Gold Rush, in February 1852, the U.S. Coast Survey published a map of every house, warehouse, wharf, street, fence, windmill, sandhill, mudflat, creek and line of vegetation in San Francisco and its environs. The astonishing degree of development above Market Street, around Yerba Buena Cove, is an enormous contrast to the nearly deserted marshlands near the mission. Market Street extended out past the line of Fremont Street in the bay. Commercial Street, past Davis Street, became Central Wharf (or as it was more commonly called, "Long Wharf") with an angle at its end to avoid running into the Market Street Wharf. Pacific and Broadway wharves headed out from Front Street to meet the ships of the world.

The isolated scatter of small structures near Mission Bay avoided the mudflats, seeking higher ground, as shown by land contours and clusters of willows and scrub oak. A slightly later version of this map, published in 1853, added hydrographic information showing Mission Bay waters to have one-foot readings until they reached an outwardly curving line from Steamboat Point on the north, to Pt. San Quentin (Potrero Point) on the south.

Mission Bay's slender connection to Gold Rush San Francisco is the Mission Plank Road (today's Mission Street), which opened as a toll road in 1851. Its three-and-a-quarter-mile length ran into trouble for the contractors where it crossed the line of Seventh Street (shown but not named on the accompanying map).

Here they had projected a bridge built on pilings, "but that plan had to be abandoned, to the astonishment and dismay of the contractor; the first pile, forty feet long, at the first blow of the pile driver sank out of sight, indicating that there was no bottom within forty feet to support a bridge. One pile having disappeared, the contractor hoisted another immediately over the first and in two blows drove the second down beyond the reach of the hammer . . . there was no foundation within eighty feet . . . pilings were abandoned, and cribs of logs were laid upon the turf so as to get a wider basis than offered by piles. The bridge made thus always shook when crossed by heavy teams and gradually settled till it was in the middle about five feet below the original level . . . the cost of the road was ninety-six thousand dollars, about thirty thousand dollars per mile . . . the plank road company obtained another franchise for a road on Folsom Street . . . in 1854 a high tide overflowed the [Folsom] road between Fourth and Fifth and floated off the planking."[35]

J.S. Hittell, writing in 1878, goes on to observe that, although these marshy areas were called swamps, "they seem to have been for part of their area at least, subterranean lakes, from forty to eighty feet deep, covered by a crust of peat moss eight or ten feet thick. . . . When the streets were first made, the weight of the sand pressed the peat down, so that the water stood where the surface was dry before. . . . More than once a contractor had put on enough sand to raise the street to the official grade, and gave notice to the city engineer to inspect the work, but in the lapse of a day between notice and inspection the sand had sunk down six or eight feet . . . heavy sand crowded under the light peat at the sides of the street and lifted it up eight or ten feet above its original level, in muddy ridges full of hideous cracks . . . it was also pushed sidewise so that houses and fences built upon it were carried away from their original position and tilted up at singular angles. . . ."

The toll road to the mission probably would have gone out Market Street, but there was an 80-foot sandhill between Second and Third streets. It wasn't long before the leveling of the city's many sandhills met the urgent need for filling in the water lots. The giant steam shovel, or "steam paddy" (it was said to do the work of twenty Irish laborers at a single stroke), started to level sandhills in 1852. It could be heard night and day, shoveling sand into open boxcars with

its railroad engine carrying the carloads on temporary tracks to dump in Yerba Buena Cove. Later, in the period from 1859 to 1873, the steam paddy took south-of-Market sand to fill Mission Bay.[36][37]

One of the most significant features on this first scientific map of Mission Bay is Steamboat Point, which marks the northern boundary of the bay. In 1852, Townsend Street fronted on the bay between Second and Third, with a hundred-foot sandhill close to Second Street. The geography of this important point of land was to influence the entire development of Mission Bay. Steamboat Point was high and dry land, edged by a relatively narrow shelf of shallow water (2–3 feet) meeting deeper water (24–30 feet) very close in. For this reason H.B. Tichenor built his marine railway from Steampoint Point out into the bay to haul up ships for repair. Tichenor bought his water lot in June 1851, at one of the Peter Smith sales, and said in his recollection to H.H. Bancroft that he paid $2,700 for this lot. By 1868 the Central Pacific was to pay $250,000 for this same point of land. Such was the importance of this location in the city's history.

A Sense of the Times

"And everybody made money, and was suddenly growing rich. . . ." So wrote the chroniclers of "The Annals of San Francisco," in 1854, trying to explain the extraordinary events they had observed and written about as publishers and editors of the city's early prestigious newspapers.[38] To understand the nature

Mission Bay, February 1852—
United States Coast Survey Map.
At the time of this topographical survey, sandhills block Market Street between Second and Third and the core of the city's development is clustered around Yerba Buena Cove, north of Market. The slender connection of the Mission Plank Road makes its way across the extensive salt marsh, starting at about the line of Sixth Street. Fourth Street ends just past Folsom at the edge of this same marsh, which is cut through by a meander of a tidal slough off Mission Bay. Steamboat Point has only a scatter of sheds to mark a place already teeming with shipbuilding on a large scale.

of the speculative schemes for Mission Bay real estate, it is first necessary to comprehend and appreciate the all-encompassing mood of San Francisco's population—a body of mostly young men set out on the adventure of their lives. The city had 459 inhabitants in the latter part of June 1847; by the close of 1849 there were somewhere between 25,000 and 30,000 people and "there was no such thing as a home to be found. Both dwellings and places of business were either common canvas tents, or small rough board shanties . . . only gambling saloons, hotels and restaurants and a few public buildings and stores had any pretentions to size, comfort, or elegance. . . . [T]he unplanked, ungraded, unformed streets (at one time moving heaps of dry sand and dust; at another, miry abysses, whose treacherous depths sucked in horse and dray, and occasionally man himself) were crowded with human beings from every corner of the universe and of every tongue—all excited and busy, plotting, speaking, working, buying and selling town lots, and beach and water lots, shiploads of every kind of assorted merchandise, the ships themselves, if they could—gold dust weighed in the hundredweights, ranches square leagues in extent with their thousands of cattle—allotments in hundreds of contemplated towns, already prettily designed and laid out on paper—and in short, speculating and gambling in every branch of modern commerce. . . . The loud voices of the eager seller and as-eager buyer—the laugh of reckless joy—the bold accents of successful speculation. . . . Fortunes were won and lost, upon that green cloth, in a twinkling of an eye. . . . The heated brain was never allowed to cool."[39]

Everyone ate in hotels, restaurants or boarding houses, as "time was too precious for anyone to stay indoors and cook his victuals." Tall tales, rumors and facts were all mixed together, in a continuous noisy conversation. Having no homes, where else could people go but to the bright lights and music of the gambling houses—saloons where the sight of bags of gold dust exchanging hands on the turn of a card was itself intoxicating. The peculiar fever-pitch of the times was heightened by the visible abundance of gold, "tables were piled with heaps of gold and silver coin, with bags of gold dust and lumps of pure metal to tempt the gazer. . . . Men had come to California for gold; and, by hook or crook, gold they would have. Therefore they staked and lost and staked and won—till in the end they were rich indeed, or penniless."[40]

The almost universal prediction was that San Francisco was destined to become a great world seaport, rivaling London and New York. The free flow of capital looked for investment. The fever of real estate speculation was fanned by the knowledge of local rents. Bayard Taylor, correspondent from the *New York Tribune*, wrote: "It may be interesting to give here a few instances of the enormous and unnatural value put upon property. . . . The Parker House rented for $110,000 yearly, at least $60,000 of which was paid by gamblers, who held nearly all of the second story. Adjoining it on the right was a canvas tent, fifteen by twenty-five feet, called "Eldorado" and occupied likewise by gamblers, which brought $40,000. On the opposite side of the Plaza [Portsmouth] a building called the 'Miner's Bank,' used by Wright & Co., brokers . . . was held at a rent of $75,000. A mercantile house paid $40,000 rent for a one-story building of twenty-feet front. . . . A friend of mine who wished to find a place for a law office was shown a cellar in the earth, about twelve feet square and six feet deep, which he could have for $250 a month. . . ."[41]

In addition to these enormous rents, the interest rates on borrowed money were running from eight to fifteen percent per month—paid in advance. "Real-estate, that but a few years before was of little more worth than an old song, now brought amazing prices. From twelve dollars for fifty-vara lots [a reference to the sales of August 1847] prices generally rose to hundreds, thousands and tens of thousands of dollars, so that large holders of such properties became sudden millionaires."[42]

San Franciscans gambling in 1851. J.D. Borthwick wrote, "There were a dozen or more tables each with a compact crowd of eager betters around it, and the whole room so filled with men that elbowing one's way between tables was a matter of difficulty. The atmosphere was hazy with tobacco smoke, and strongly impregnated with the fumes of brandy. . . . Nothing was heard but the slight hum of voices, and the constant clinking of money."

Plans for the Land

As the Coast Survey Map shows the actual level of development in San Francisco and Mission Bay, so the 1853 map by Alex Zakreski delineates the plans for the land—a look at the future.

Among the planned extensions and improvements are the water lots from Brannan Street south, past Channel Street, around Steamboat Point (mislabeled Pt. San Quentin by Zakreski, who took the then-current name from more southern Potrero Point) up to Rincon Point. Mission Creek and Channel Street (in Mission Bay) mark the southern boundary of the city; the presidio defines the northern limits as "Government Reserve." The grid pattern of streets, laid out in O'Farrell's 1847 survey, extends right out into the shallow coves of the bay, defining the boundaries of water lots.

Already the precedent had been set with Kearny's "Great Sale of Beach and Water Lots" in Yerba Buena Cove in 1847. As Congress had transferred "swamplands and tidelands to the state of Arkansas and *other states*" in an act in 1851, these rectangles of land under water represented State of California lands, now conveyed by an act of the state legislature to San Francisco—with some provisos. The act required that the city pay the state 25 percent of the value of the water lots sold, and also gave the city the land for only 99 years, a long-term lease that enabled the state to sell water lot "reversionary rights" a second time around. As a result we find the same land being auctioned first by the city and some months later by the state, resulting in future confusion of title. Buyers of "reversionary rights" (property their heirs would not own until 1950–51) could use these titles for speculative purposes.

The city of San Francisco plunged into debt making street improvements of heroic proportions, paying city contractors in city scrip (promissory notes) for which water lots now became collateral. City scrip bore the relatively modest interest rate of three percent a month—still, that amounted to 36 percent a

The plan for San Francisco in 1853. *Zakreski's map is entitled, "The only correct & fully complete Map of San Francisco, Compiled from the Original Map & recent Surveys, Containing all the latest extensions & improvements, New streets, alleys, places, wharfs & Divisions of Wards. Respectfully dedicated to the City Authorities. 1853"*

year, causing modest debts to bloom into substantial amounts. One of the city's contractors was Dr. Peter Smith.

The Infamous Dr. Peter Smith—Dr. Peter Smith is one of the elusive characters of the Gold Rush who appears in San Francisco in 1850 and is gone by 1854, never to be mentioned again except in newspaper accounts and in the ensuing legal snarls over land titles, where his name is always coupled with "infamous." It all started fairly innocently.

In 1850, Dr. Peter Smith contracted with San Francisco to care for the sick among the city's indigent population at the rate of $4 per day per patient, to be paid in city scrip at the customary 3 percent interest per month. In 1851 Dr. Smith demanded that his city scrip be exchanged for coin; he went to court and obtained a judgment against the city for $19,238 (out of an eventual total of $64,431). Under a law that allowed creditors to sell property belonging to their debtors, Dr. Smith coerced the city fathers (now called "The Commission for the Funded Debt") into selling available San Francisco real estate, mostly water lots, to pay off his claims. Meanwhile the state legislature passed an enabling bill so that San Francisco could convert its scrip into bonds bearing 10 percent per annum. Smith was not agreeable to exchanging his scrip for bonds, he wanted cash.

The first great Peter Smith sale took place on June 14, 1851, as Sheriff Jack Hayes auctioned 103 water lots, seven blocks of beachfront property and seven additional lots belonging to the city. That same day, a notice signed by all the members of Commission for the Funded Debt appeared in the newspapers: ". . . the public is hereby notified that the city has no legal title to said lots. . . . Everyone will readily perceive that a purchase made at the Sheriff's sale will convey no title. . . ."[43]

It is hardly surprising that, although the lots were all sold, the prices were "not a twentieth or even a fiftieth part of their value." As not enough money was raised to pay Smith's debt, a second auction was held on July 8. Still the cloud of "no title conveyed" hung over the properties, requiring a third, a fourth and, on January 30, 1852, a great final sale in which 2,000 acres of city land were disposed of.

By now everyone realized that, whether the city fathers were deliberately depressing the prices of the water lots so they could buy up the land for themselves and friends, or whether they had simply bungled one attempt after another to make good their debt to Dr. Smith, the fact was that they had sold off "the patrimony of the city" for very little return. None of this was accomplished quietly. The newspapers of the city took sides, attacking or defending State Senator David Broderick, who fathered many of the water lot bills in Sacramento and at the same time bought bargain lots in San Francisco.

In time, the matter of whether the buyers at the Peter Smith sales held clear title to their land went to the California Supreme Court where the surprising unanimous decision was reached that the titles were valid. One of the judges was the same man who earlier, as learned counsel to the Commission for the Funded Debt, had advised that body to publish his opposite opinion. Dr. Smith took his settlement and title to 75 of the lots and left town. Later in a series of decisions, the Supreme Court of the United States set aside the California court's action.

One outcome of the Peter Smith sales was a spate of investment and speculation in South Beach and Mission Bay water lots. Two men who profited much were "Judge" John McHenry and William Cornell Jewett.

McHenry and Jewett: Mission Bay Speculators—Self-styled "Judge" John McHenry arrived in San Francisco on board the ship *Northerner* on August 15, 1850. In 1854 John McHenry was a Montgomery Street lawyer at 12 Armory Hall.[44] By then he had turned a handsome profit in Mission Bay real estate,

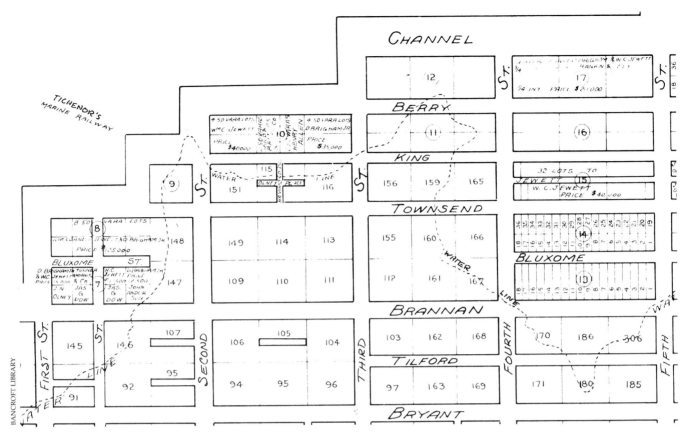

"Map of South Beach Water Property, showing purchases made by Wm. Cornell Jewett . . . Sept. 1st, 1853." Only a portion of Jewett's property is shown on this part of the map. South Beach Blocks 7 and 8 are bounded by First and Second streets between Townsend and Brannan, and intersected by Bluxome and Eaker. The dotted "water-line" represents the 1853 shoreline. South-of-Market blocks are 820 feet long and 360 feet wide, including the narrow, intersecting alleys that allowed for more frontage. Water lots varied in size and shape according to their location. For example, Block 13 measures 820 feet in length but only about 265 in width. In this instance individual parcels were 45.5 feet wide and 132 feet deep, for a total of 36 per water lot.

buying low at Peter Smith sales and selling high. In one instance he picked up lots the second time around when the original buyers defaulted on payment. The south waterfront property that the *Alta California* opined "was not worth a brass farthing" in 1852, dangled price tags in the thousands by 1853. By tracing the transactions on two water lots, South Beach Blocks 7 and 8, we can better understand why the cost of Mission Bay property spiraled upwards.

Blocks 7 and 8 appear on a map drawn for William Cornell Jewett on September 1, 1853, to show his South Beach property. (A portion of this map is shown above). What is unusual about Jewett's map is that lots are identified not only by owner but by price.

South Beach Blocks numbered 7 and 8 are bounded by First and Second streets, and Brannan and Townsend, just north of where Tichenor's marine railway juts out into the bay at the foot of Second Street on Block 9. H.B. Tichenor paid $2,700 for Block 9 at a Peter Smith auction in 1851; he recollects his price as the highest paid at that sale for an individual lot on the south waterfront.[45] Jewett's price on half of the adjoining Block 8 rose to $125,000 by 1853.

San Francisco's early books of recorded deeds reveal that South Beach Blocks 7 and 8 were sold by Dr. Peter Smith to John McHenry on June 15, 1851, in a package that included Mission Bay water lot 20, plus other water lots numbering 316, 319, 352 and 580. All sold for a total of $3,795. In the deed Smith states that "these same lots and parcels of land were this day conveyed to me by John Hayes, Sheriff. . . ." In this instance Sheriff Hayes conveyed parcels directly to Peter Smith rather than putting them up for auction. John McHenry picked up Blocks 7 and 8 for a prorated cost of $542.50 each. On September 1, 1853, McHenry turned a fancy profit by selling Blocks 7 and 8—each containing eight 50-vara lots, to William Cornell Jewett for $50,000.[46]

As the deeds do not record the terms of payment, we cannot know how much of Jewett's $50,000 was credit and how much cash, but on that same day he conveyed two of the eight water lots on Blocks 7 to new owners, one to James Dow for $15,000 and another to D. Brigham for $10,000.[47] Later that week, on September 6, he sold John Anderson and David Turner each a 50-vara lot for $7,500. By September 15, his sale to A. Carle of another lot on Block 7 for $10,000 returned his original purchase price of $50,000. Now Jewett owned all of Block 8 free and clear. On the 20th he sold another water lot on Block 7 to J.N. Olney for $10,000 and on September 24, H.A. Allen paid him $5,500 for half a 50-vara water lot on Block 7.

On his map (dated September 1, 1853) Jewett offered his holdings in Block 8 for $125,000—eight 50-vara water lots for $15,625 each. Whatever he sold them for, these transactions were all clear profit. By October 1854 Jewett no longer owned any land on these two water lot blocks. Only one of the 1853 lot-holders' names remains in place, that of James Olney.[48]

For buyers like John McHenry and William C. Jewett, the controversy over clear titles worked to their risky advantage. They were in early and cheap and realized their profit long before the Peter Smith titles were cleared, then canceled by successive court actions. Jewett gambled: since his buyers were speculating as well, he could shuffle deeds around with the hope that he would not own these parcels at a time their titles might be declared invalid.

Jewett followed this same speculative pattern on Mission Bay water lots 20 and 22. He actually made about $20,000 on a block he priced at $40,000 on his 1853 map. Every buyer must have been convinced he got a bargain. Jewett's map showing both price and ownership served two purposes: it inflated values, and the published names of so many active investors on this nearly empty southern waterfront suggested a prosperous future.

One interesting aspect of Jewett's Mission Bay investments is that he built his own home on Lot 115, between Townsend and King, Second and Third streets. The Jewett residence would have been on a rise of land (shown as Lime Hill on his deed) overlooking Mission Bay, at a time when virtually no other homes were there. It predated the beginnings of nearby South Park by three years. There was not even a good road to his home from his office on Merchant at Masonic Hall, where he is listed as broker in 1854. Four lots, including Jewett's home, were deeded to his wife, Almira Jewett, on June 7, 1853, as a "token of my goodwill, affection and esteem."[49] Thus Jewett effectively protected his home from suits, liens and costly controversy, and controversy was his way of life.

William Cornell Jewett arrived in San Francisco on May 27, 1849, as noted in the Society of California Pioneers Register. Unlike other 49'ers, he was accompanied by his wife, described as "surely the most beautiful woman in California," by a portrait painter of San Francisco society who noted in a letter dated February 1850 that Jewett and Almira would sit for him, as "anyone who is anyone is painted by William S. Jewett." The coincidence of name is just that; they were not related.[50]

On April 3, 1856, California's Governor Johnson appointed William C. Jewett as notary public (one of 21 such appointees in California) and twenty days later he sought to remove both Jewett and another notary, James Bristow (also of San Francisco), from their positions. In *The People rel. Finlay* v. *Jewett,* the California Supreme Court upheld Jewett's right to complete his term of office. However, after 1856 Jewett is no longer listed in San Francisco city directories.

His brief biography describes him as "a publicist and peace advocate," noting that Jewett was so opposed to the Civil War that he traveled to Europe and "harried European potentates and premiers with his personal telegraphic and epistolary communications." He spent much of the rest of his life in Canada, avoiding arrest for his anti-Union activities, and he died in Switzerland in 1893.[51]

The speculative activities of both Jewett and McHenry were the beginning of a web of business deals set up to profit on land still under water in Mission Bay. Jewett is unusual in that he built his house as close to his water lot real estate as possible. It is a matter of conjecture whether he did it to be a more effective salesman on the spot, or because he anticipated that boom that was ten years in the future in this part of the waterfront.

MEXICAN LAND CLAIMS: THE U.S. LAND COMMISSION AND THE BURDEN OF PROOF, 1851–1854

Commodore John Sloat promised the Mexican-Californians to guarantee their land titles. The pledge was repeated by military governors General Stephen Kearny and Colonel Richard Mason, and backed up in 1848 by the treaty of Guadalupe Hidalgo, which gave the resident Mexicans their American citizenship. In the excitement of the Gold Rush, from 1848 to 1850, the whole question of Mexican land titles was put aside. But in anticipation of legal questions that were bound to arise, confidential agents of the United States combed the archives (then in considerable disarray) of the California missions and in Mexico City for some semblance of land surveys and documents that could be used as legal proof in United States courts.

The documents were assembled in one place and finally collected into 300 books of 800 pages each, "some pages worn and stained, a few with musket holes shot through," but the original subject indexes were disregarded.[52] Their generally haphazard rearrangement meant that papers relating to the missions might turn up in military matters, and questions regarding land grants might be anywhere, in any order. Most of the documents were in Spanish and there was much disagreement in American legal circles as to intentions and meanings of various phrases. This might not have been so important had it not turned out that paper claims were the basis for most of the legal decisions that confirmed or denied titles.

Hoping to settle the messy problem of Mexican land claims in California, Congress created the U.S. Land Commission. Appointed in March of 1851, the three commissioners with their support staff (only one could read Spanish) were to serve for three years. By then, it was hoped, the tangle of land ownership of these large Mexican grants would be unsnarled, if not to everyone's satisfaction, at least without bloodshed. The life of the U.S. Land Commission was extended to 1856, but some of the titles were still the subject of dispute in courts in 1880.[53]

The burden of proof of ownership lay on the claimants, who had to travel to San Francisco within a specified time and present their claims, papers, and witnesses to the commission. If the commission's decisions had been final, with no appeal, the process might not have ruined the claimants. But now, as American citizens, they had the right of appeal to the U.S. District Court, and on up to the U.S. Supreme Court, as did all third parties. "In nearly every case, whatever might have been the decision of the Land Commission, an appeal was taken."[54]

"The native Californians suddenly surrounded by a strange population, strange laws, a strange language, strange customs, and strange industries, were virtually deprived of the bulk of their wealth, and then compelled to raise money to defend themselves against complete spoliation by the government. . . . Nor did the trouble and expense come to an end when he had gained his case in the Land Commission. As boundaries as well as titles were in dispute, the Americans who wanted to buy farms . . . were afraid to pay for deeds in which they could have no confidence. Under compulsion . . . they became squatters, that is they seized and occupied as their own, land claimed under Mexican grant. Having once made their settlement, they acquired interests which they defended in the courts. If they could defeat the Mexican grants they could acquire the land for a trifle. They were numerous, and became a political power. . . . There were squatter governors, squatter legislatures and a squatter press."[55]

The two large Mexican claims to the Potrero were those of José Cornelio Bernal to the *Potrero Viejo* (Islais Creek Basin and Hunters Point) and the de Haro family to the *Potrero Neuvo* (several thousand acres between Mission Creek and Mission Bay on the north, down to and including Potrero Point on the south). On August 4, 1857, a portion amounting to 826.44 of the original 4,442 acres of the Bernal rancho grant, *Rincon de las Salinas y Potrero Viejo* was confirmed to the Bernal heirs. Another small plot of 5.86 acres was also confirmed to the Bernal claimants on July 27, 1863.[56] The de Haro claim remained in the courts until 1868. Meanwhile, would-be settlers populated Mission Bay land, fencing in lots for small farms and putting up modest homes.

By the time a squatter had raised his family in a home built on disputed land in the Potrero in the early 1850s, the possibility that he might one day be dispossessed must have seemed less and less likely. However, a newspaper item that appeared in the *Alta* on June 8, 1854, would have been unnerving: "An important motion was entertained yesterday by the U.S. Land Commission in the Potrero case, and one apparently vital to the decision of this valuable claim, in which many of our citizens and property holders are largely interested. The claim had been filed in the Secretary's office in due time; and the counsel for the claimant now allege that a few months ago they discovered in an old batch of papers in the Mission, an original grant of the land made in 1840 by Micheltorrena to the de Haros. The motion made now is to amend the record by admitting this paper on file, which, if it proves genuine—and there is some strong testimony to its genuineness—confirms the claim beyond a doubt. The motion was not decided."

The same paper on the same day: "Another squatter affair took place yesterday morning, about ten o'clock, at the corner of First and Howard streets, nearly opposite the late squatter riot. The Marshal received information that a party of men who were armed were fencing in the lot, and immediately proceeded to the spot with a force of police, where he found a man named Peter McKinney engaged in fencing in a lot. . . . McKinney had brandished a pistol and threatened to shoot anyone who interfered with him."

"Hope deferred maketh the heart sick," editorialized the *Alta* in September 1854. "Some months ago, the city of San Francisco was in a state of turmoil and excitement, resulting from the encroachments of squatters. Life as well as property was in danger, nightly riots and brawls disturbed the peace." The hope of the *Alta* was for speedy decisions by the Land Commission to settle boundary disputes of the city.

With the fury of a man who has witnessed the process that worked for no one but lawyers, Bancroft wrote in 1882: "It was to the Californians owning lands under genuine and valid titles, seven eighths of the claimants . . . that great wrong was done. They were virtually robbed by the government that was bound to protect them. As a rule, they lost nearly all their possessions in the struggle before the successive tribunals to escape from real and imaginary dangers of total loss. The lawyers took immense fees in land and cattle, often for slight service or none at all. It was in no sense the protection promised by the treaty to finally confirm a title after a struggle of eight to twenty-five years when half or all of the estate had passed from the possession of the original claimant; it was simply confiscation, and that not in the real interests of the United States, or of American settlers, but of speculating land sharpers."[57]

It was the considered opinion of most observers that if the 700 valid claims had been confirmed immediately, the owners of these ranchos (who were invariably hard pressed for cash) would have gladly sold small tracts to settlers for homes and farms at the most reasonable prices. The continuing uncertainty about the ownership of the lands of the Potrero and Mission Bay was prolonged until the late 1860s; meanwhile squatters moved on to the vacant land. "Every occupant felt that his possession was threatened by squatters on the one hand or by grant-owners on the other; neither the squatters or the grant-owners could sell, or dared to invest in expensive improvements, thus population was driven away, industry was stifled."[58]

A Confidential Letter from Jasper O'Farrell—This previously unpublished letter from the California Historical Society file of surveyor Jasper O'Farrell suggests that internal machinations within claimants' families may have added to the legal complications on these large land grants.

"Confidential to Friend MacCorkle, Sonoma City," from Jasper O'Farrell, dated "Wednesday, 7 Dec. 10 am/ 18--" [1859, or 1864 by perpetual calendar]: *". . . F. de Haro was a Sergt. in the troop of Col. Vallejo some 26 years ago when he was Commandante de Yerba Buena. The Sgt. had a wife— young and beautiful—for possession and enjoyment of whose charms the Col. yearned but in vain. The husband's presence kept the wife true and virtuous, it was necessary to get rid of him in some way. Gov. Alvarado (a nephew of the Col.) had to transmit dispatches to his government in Mexico. Sgt. de Haro was recommended by his Col. and was appointed and accepted the honorable and responsible position as envoy with tears of gratitude; leaving his young wife and two children under the protection of his* **dear friend**—*the Commandante. The consequence was the wife . . . was seduced and before [de Haro's] return (but about twelve months after his departure) was delivered of twin daughters which were easily palmed off on the poor Sgt. as his own by adding a few months to their age upon his return. . . . Some seven or eight years ago the Legislature of California passed a law making females of 18 . . . competent . . . it was [passed?] through the legislature by agents of the Col. (now General). The twins above mentioned were heiress to a valuable tract of land near San Francisco (El Potrero); the General wanted it. The girls were the age mentioned in the law and were made competent by the law to sell their property. . . . The General had an interview with them and, base of all baseness, informed them of their Mother's shame. And that he, not de Haro was the author of their birth. Their Mother was dead. They . . . were being educated by the Sisters of Notre Dame at San Jose . . . they were high minded, educated and refined. Can you imagine the depth of his infamy—to destroy the happiness of innocent children. . . . It was* **necessary** *that his advice as* **Father** *be followed so they sold the Potrero . . . for one fourth its value. Do you see the motive? I do!. . . . could he by a little maneuvering . . . have the lion's share. . . ? I can convince him of the utter hopelessness of the heirs of the de Haros ever being able to sustain a successful suit. . . ."[59]*

In this last statement, O'Farrell's prediction was accurate. Other aspects of the letter are also correct. A census of inhabitants in San Francisco in 1842 lists Francisco de Haro as being 50 years old with eleven children, apparently a recent widower, as he has an infant son. Twin girls listed as Cadria and Carlotta are aged nine, putting their births in 1833 (depending on the month they were born and the precise dates of the census).

The *California Statutes* state in 1854, "Males shall be deemed of full and legal age when they shall be 21 and females when they shall be 18 years old. Males and females of legal age as fixed by this act shall be competent to . . . convey real estate. . . ."[61]

Vallejo was commandante of the San Francisco Company in 1831–32, but the question of de Haro's whereabouts is less easily ascertained. In 1831–32 de Haro is listed as *"Suplente of the diputacion,"* which, however, does not enable us to precisely fix his location.[62] Whether de Haro was in Mexico for a year at that time is debatable. He was not in the army, having resigned in 1824, but he would have been available for such a mission by virtue of his education and his record of public service. Further research may answer some of these unresolved questions.

TWENTY-ONE

The 1857 Coast Survey Map, Showing Mission Bay. *In the five-year period since the earlier Coast Survey map, the most eye-catching change is the proliferation of truck gardens around the Mission Dolores (lower-left corner). Mission Creek continues its meander undisturbed. Brannan Street fronts on the remains of the salt marsh from Fourth Street to Ninth, where it bridges Mission Creek. Mission Plank Road now has a twin toll road, Folsom Road, which makes the "O'Farrell Swing" to the south, toward Mission Dolores.*

Features on the map are discussed in the text that follows. For their modern location see the modern aerial with historic overlay.

Rincon

MARKET

South Park

Brannan

MISSION BAY

Steamboat Point

Mission Rock

EARLY DEVELOPMENT AROUND MISSION BAY, 1850-1857

At the time of the Gold Rush, the Mission Dolores was in a sleepy, country setting where Mission Creek meandered through marshes to the broad expanse of Mission Bay. The marshes were the most popular places for duck hunters, who could count on bagging more birds in one hour than they could carry on horseback to the city. Just beyond the mission, a freshwater spring fed a stream lined with willows. This bucolic setting was a great contrast to the muddy, teeming streets and windswept sandhills of the city.

Two would-be developers, Dr. John Townsend and Cornelius de Boom, envisioned San Francisco's first suburb on the south bank of Mission Creek. The site was a mile closer to the city and considerably more inviting than a projected Hunters Point development. In 1849 they drew up a grid of streets and offered the land for sale. As there were no families wanting small homes and no road leading to the city, no more was heard of this planned development after 1850. We do not know its precise location beyond " the south bank of Mission Creek."[63] Dr. Townsend and de Boom appear to have had no clear title to the land they hoped to sell, but they must have assumed that empty land should be put to good use.

The beginning of commercial enterprise on Mission Creek was in response to a booming San Francisco market: a brickyard and distillery were the first manufacturing concerns on the creek. Their exact locations are hazy and neither can be located with certainty on the 1852 or the 1857 Coast Survey maps. The bricks were made of clay found on the creek banks and loaded on shallow-draft boats to sail with the tide. Bricks were in great demand in the city as a result of the disastrous fires of the early 1850s but local builders preferred the superior fired products that arrived from England and the East Coast as ballast on incoming ships. Even less is known about the distillery; in 1878 it was remembered as being at the head of Mission Creek in 1855, from where one could see "the schooners that sailed up and down, loaded with lumber, fuel, bricks, grain and whiskey."[64]

It was in 1854, to accommodate to this shipping, that the state legislators designated Mission Creek a navigable stream, and in 1855 they granted a franchise for a bridge across the creek from Brannan Street to Potrero Avenue, with a proviso that the bridge should not obstruct the free navigation of the creek.[65]

Mission Bay's isolation from the city is emphasized by an 1853 request made by several factory owners who asked the Board of Aldermen to set aside an area south of Mission Creek for a proposed industrial zone "so remote from the inhabited part of the city that no legal question would likely arise as to what might constitute a nuisance in the district, at least within the period named in the ordinance, until January 1, 1869." The factory owners ran slaughter houses and the area they had in mind was near Ninth and Brannan, on the creek. This became the early "Butchers' Reserve" by city ordinance. The butchers chose this location because the tidal waters from Mission Bay flushed the area twice a day, washing away the waste that was swept through their trap doors. The south-of-Market boys recall supplying patients from the hospital at Sixth and Brannan (French Benevolent Hospital) with "healthy, warm animal blood, at 10 cents a cup, from the slaughter houses on Mission Creek."[66] The butchers remained on Brannan Street between Sixth and Ninth streets until 1870, when another city ordinance moved them farther south to First and Kentucky; this time they used Islais Creek for their waste disposal.[67]

Mission Dolores, 1851. By 1851–52 the "old Mission" had become the goal of many a San Francisco outing at the end of Mission Road. A picturesque remnant of the Spanish past, the delapidated church had a number of public houses and gambling saloons close by so that culture could be combined with refreshment of a lower order.

Early Potrero Point Enterprises—Another nuisance-industry ordinance passed by the San Francisco aldermen on May 9, 1853, prohibited the storage of gunpowder within the city limits. As a result, the storeship *Dryade*, moored at the foot of Telegraph Hill, was removed "two miles from town, where in the winter the wind blows heavily and renders it impossible to load the boat without wetting the powder."[68] On the Coast Survey Map of 1857, the windy, winter anchorage of the *Dryade* can be found on the southeastern tip of Point San Quentin (Potrero Point) at the Powder Works. Two deepwater wharves extend out to where ships can load their dangerous product. The powder works of the mid-1850s were both isolated and substantial. In two-story brick structures measuring fifty by thirty feet, with walls twelve inches thick, the powder was stored that eventually blasted away many of San Francisco's famous hills.

Another early Potrero industry can be found on the 1857 Coast Survey Map on Potrero Point, near the powder works. A dark diagonal line labeled "Rope Walk" extends over a marsh and ends at a wharf. This is the 1856 Tubbs Cordage Company that was in the business of importing hemp from Manilla and twisting strands into ropes for use in shipping and mines. The Rope Walk was a one-story wooden shed, 35 feet high and 1000 feet long, used by workmen who twisted strands of abaca fibers into ropes as they walked backward along the rope walk. Hardly a nuisance industry, Tubbs Cordage was unusual in its need to cut diagonally through two blocks of land near the waterfront. The southern side of Potrero Point afforded both cheap land and deep-water anchorage that the manufactory required. The company prospered and grew in the 1880s and '90s, when they exported rope to South America.

Vegetable Gardens, Race Tracks and Pleasure Gardens—After the first San Francisco survey in 1852, the Coast Survey Map of 1857 demonstrates a major change in the countryside around the Mission Dolores (as it was popularly called). Open lands have become cultivated gardens. Where Folsom and Mission streets turn south (at Eleventh and Twelfth streets today), patterned squares and rectangles abut each other on the map and completely surround the mission with fields of produce raised for a population of 78,000 to the north. Much of the 1852 swampland of Mission Bay had been reclaimed as vegetable gardens in the land between Folsom and Harrison, near Sixth Street.

Near the mission there was fresh water for irrigation and cheap land that was frequently used rather than owned by the produce farmers. There were now two good roads—Mission and Folsom—for wagon delivery to the city's markets. Windmills can be found on the 1857 map as small symbols shaped like Maltese crosses. From the 1850s through the 1870s the gardens in the Mission Bay district

San Francisco From Above. *An 1854 birdseye view of San Francisco shows the tidal arm of Mission Creek winding inland from Mission Bay (far left) and the isolated settlement of Mission Dolores beyond. Steamboat Point marks the outer entrance to Mission Bay. The central oval of South Park's garden has been constructed one block north of Steamboat Point. Development of the city was concentrated north of Market Street, seen here reaching out as a wharf into the bay.*

Russ Garden. Topiary gates twined with flowers and flying flags welcomed a stage from the Omnibus Line, gentlemen on horseback and smart, low-slung landaus, ladiies with their parasols, Chinese carrying produce baskets, and couples on foot. Music could be heard from the canvas tent that covered the dance pavilion as groups of gymnasts performed amazing feats for anyone with the small admission price.

were farmed largely by Chinese, who delivered produce to the city markets and also went from door to door in the better neighborhoods of Rincon Hill and South Park carrying baskets of fresh vegetables swinging from their shoulders. San Francisco's hotels and restaurants carried on a lively trade and were said to rival Paris and New York in the quality of exotic variety of their menus. Venison and game came from Marin County, butter from Point Reyes, vegetables from Mission Bay gardens and ducks from the marshes, nearby.

During the 1850s the Mission Dolores became a picturesque reminder of an earlier life, the perfect goal for a Sunday outing. Public houses and gambling saloons opened nearby to take care of the trade—"the Grizzly Bear House, the Half-Way House, Milk Punch House, the Nightengale [sic] and the Noantum House," to name a few from 1854. The course of the Union Race Track can be found just south of the mission and farther south (beyond this section of the map) was the Pioneer Race Track. The tracks were built here because of a shared conviction that horses ran faster on a wet, springy turf. In 1850, between Twentieth and Twenty-fourth streets, Mr. A.A. Greene built the first regulation track. San Francisco's racetracks were described as "probably not surpassed by any in the world, where especially on Sunday . . . the most celebrated of the fleet steeds of California are matched against each other to the delight of the multitude."[69] By 1852, horses were being brought in from Australia to race California horses on these fast tracks.

For those whose taste ran more to dancing and dining in a bucolic setting, there was the "Willows." François Pioche, a French capitalist, built the Willows in a small meadow watered by a stream lined with willow trees (located on the 1857 map between Seventeenth and Nineteenth streets, Valencia and Mission Road). Dances were held in the outdoor pavilion and the willow trees offered pleasant seclusion for outdoor dining. The little resort was very popular with San Franciscans, who could ride out the Mission Plank Road on afternoon excursions and enjoy the warmer weather and the sight of full-grown trees. The Willows sat on land some twenty feet lower than its surroundings, and in 1861 it was flooded, never to reopen. (Bancroft notes that the small freshwater lake described by the mission fathers as the site of their first encampment would have been where the Willows stood in later years.)

Another popular public garden was Russ's Gardens, seen on the 1857 map at Simmons (Sixth Street) and Folsom. Christian Russ, who made his money in jewelry and real estate speculation during the Gold Rush, opened his family estate to the entire German population of San Francisco on May 1, 1853.d An estimated 1,800 Germans "danced, sang, drank, smoked and made merry, as only such an enthusiastic race of mortals could."[70] Russ proceeded to invite the French to celebrate on Bastille Day, the Irish to drink to St. Patrick and the Yankee population to parade to his gardens on the 4th of July. Russ's Gardens, for a small fee, was open to all.

In the first years of the Gold Rush people had little time or opportunity for fresh-air outings. The most popular activity was to climb Telegraph Hill and look at the bay, a truly spectacular sight with its "forest of masts," something never seen before or since. But as life settled down in the mid-1850s and families with children became more common, the need was obvious for "places to take the air" with some trees or gardens.

In their hurry to divide city land and sell it to each other, the city fathers had entertained no notion of public spaces. Portsmouth Square was a disgrace, as described by a visiting Englishman, Hinton R. Helper: ". . . it is nothing more or less than a cow-pen, enclosed with unplaned plank. . . . In the middle is planted a tall liberty-pole, near which is erected a rude rostrum for lynch-lawyers and noisy politicians. If there is a tree, or a bush, or a shrub, or a sprig of grass, or anything else in or about it that is green . . . nobody has ever seen it; and, as a pleasure ground, it is used only by the four-footed denizens of the city."[71]

The annalists of San Francisco summed up the state of affairs in 1854: "Over all these square miles of contemplated thoroughfares, there seems no provision made by the projectors for a public park—the true 'lungs' of a large city. The existing plaza, or Portsmouth Square, and two or three other diminutive squares delineated on the plan, seem the only breathing-holes intended for the future population of hundreds of thousands. This is a strange mistake, and can only be attributed to the jealous avarice of the city projectors in turning every square *vara* of the site into an available building lot. Indeed, the eye is wearied, and the imagination quite stupefied in looking over the numberless square—all square—building blocks and mathematically straight lines of streets, miles long, and every one crossing a host of others at right angles. . . . Not only is there no public park or garden but there is not even a circus, oval, open terrace, broad avenue, or any ornamental line of street or building, or verdant space of any kind, other than the three or four small squares alluded to; and which every resident knows are by no means verdant, except in patches where stagnant water collects and ditch weeds grow."[72]

As if in answer to the annalists whose work was published in 1854, South Park was the first planned neighborhood in the city; it was designed in the shape of an oval, around an enclosed garden. Started in 1855 by George Gordon, a British real-estate developer, on what was described as "the only level spot of land free from sand in the city limits," South Park had a central fenced garden, planted with yew trees that were still of spindly proportions in 1861. Elegant townhouses—narrow, two-story brick buildings with stone facings on their corners—started on the north side of the park but never advanced much beyond a third of the planned oval. The first residents included upper-echelon army and navy officers, social-minded southerners, and well-to-do commission merchants. Gordon had the bad luck to have attempted his planned garden townhouses at the very moment San Francisco had its first financial crisis and real-estate values plummeted. By the time things had recovered, the Second Street cut had devalued Rincon Hill to the north, and finished any social gloss on south of Market real-estate ventures. South Park exists today, although its townhouses are long gone. It runs from Second to Third streets, between Bryant and Brannan. The houses shown in this 1865 woodcut are approximately the same as found on the 1857 Coast Survey map.

South Park Party. *A welcome to the Russian Fleet, celebrated the victory of the Crimean War with a tent party ball at South Park. A windmill in the center of the oval irrigated the forlorn yew trees. Only a third of elegant rowhouses were completed as planned. Mission Bay lies in the distance.*

STEAMBOAT POINT, 1851-1864

The most important early industry on Mission Bay gave its name to the point of land bounded by Second Street on the northeast, and just short of the line of Fourth Street on the southwest, with Townsend Street marking the edge of the bay in 1852.

By 1851, although there were suddenly hundreds of vessels of all sizes and types operating in and out of San Francisco, the city had no facility for hauling or drydocking vessels for bottom-cleaning, caulking, coppering or other repairs below the waterline. To meet this obvious need, Henry B. Tichenor constructed a marine railway at the foot of Second Street in 1851. Then as now, a marine railway consisted of tracks laid out into the water from above the high-tide line. To haul a vessel out of the water, it was maneuvered onto a stout iron-wheeled cradle that was drawn up the inclined railway by a windlass or capstan. Tichenor's lot, partly land and partly water, with access to deep water close at hand, was ideally suited for ship repair.

As early as 1849, knocked-down steamboats were being shipped to San Francisco from the East, to be put back together again on the beach at Happy Valley (from Market Street south to Rincon Point). Domingo Marcuci—who had come out with the pieces of the *Captain Sutter* and accompanying shipwrights, engineers, and captain—put the vessel together in six weeks at the foot of Folsom Street. Before long, in the early 1850s, he moved to Steamboat Point, around Fourth and King. Here he built the ships *Reliance*, *Cyrus Walker*, *Flora Templeton* and probably the barkentine *Monitor*. Later, from 1866 to 1869, he used Tichenor's Second Street ways to build the sternwheeler *Pioneer*, the propellor *Santa Cruz* and the big steam *Vallejo*.

John G. North established his boatyard at Steamboat Point about 1854 "on the south side of Townsend, between Third and Fourth." The noblest vessel ever to be launched from Steamboat Point, the sidewheeler *Chrysopolis*, came from North's yard in 1860, before he moved to the Potrero. She was the biggest steamer ever built at San Francisco up to that date, the grandest of the floating palaces of the California river trades and the all-time speed queen of the Sacramento riverboats. North is said to have built 53 steamboats and 220 vessels of other types, including the first three-masted schooner on the Pacific Coast, the *Susan and Kate Denin*, launched at Steamboat Point in 1854.[73]

Another famous and prolific Steamboat Point builder was Patrick Henry Tiernan, one of whose earliest jobs at San Francisco involved converting the steamer *Goliath* to tugboat service at Steamboat Point. At Third and King between 1856 and 1858, Tiernan built the sidewheeler *Paul Pry*, the sternwheeler *Peytonia*, and the steamers *Petaluma* and *Sophia McLean*. Around Fourth and Townsend between 1859 and 1861, he built the sternwheelers *Visalia* and *Swallow* and the sidewheelers *Sacramento* and *Oakland*. Apparently moving back and forth between a Fourth

Launching the Camanche, November 14, 1864: *The monitor* Camanche, *shipped out from New Jersey in pieces, was put together at Third and King by mechanics of Peter Donahue's Union Iron Works. Her armor plate was eleven inches thick around the turret. Her launching place is the site of one of John North's earlier shipyards.*

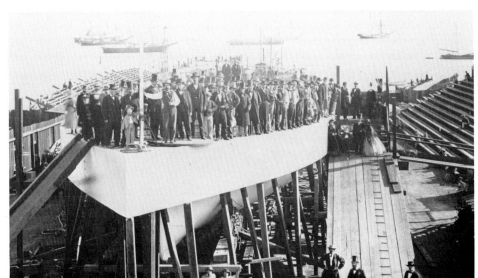

Tichenor's Ways, the Foot of Second Street. *The marine railway at the foot of Second Street began operations in 1851. Ships coming onto these ways, such as the brigantine* Hesperian, *shown here in 1862, would be repaired and launched into the deep water beyond. Mules were used to turn the capstan—the large, circular device in the foreground—which hauled the ship up the ways and out of the water.*

Street and Third Street location, he built in 1862-1864 the steamers *Banner, Esmerelda, Governor Dana* and *Julia,* together with a number of barges. Then he, too, moved out to the Potrero, complaining, as had North, that Steamboat Point didn't have enough elbowroom anymore. In 1870 he revisited the foot of Second Street to supervise the building of the Southern Pacific's huge railroad-car ferry *Thoroughfare.*[74]

Although no photographs of Steamboat Point in the Gold Rush period have thus far appeared, photographs from the early 1860s give us a very good idea of what shipbuilding involved. It must be emphasized that these early shipbuilders constructed even the largest class of riverboats—equivalents of the floating palaces on the Mississippi and Hudson rivers—in starkly unimproved surroundings. All that was required for a "shipyard" was proximity to water and a sliver of flat land big enough to set up a vessel. Materials and craftsmen and the "master builder" were really what constituted a shipyard.

Steamboat Point is important to the rest of Mission Bay's development in this period of the 1850s because ships were the carriers of all the city's trade. It was at Steamboat Point that they were repaired and built as major capital investments by the city's most prominent citizens. Important men, on important business—commission merchants, brokers, traders and sea captains—dropped in to oversee the building and repair of their ships. It was at John North's yard, for example, that William Ralston, the city's biggest banker who lent money to the men who built many of San Francisco's industrial enterprises, had his favorite yacht, the *Brisk,* cut in two and lengthened.

San Francisco's capitalists clearly understood, "The city will be forced to spread over the extensive and comparatively level tract of ground lying to the southwest, on the banks of Mission Creek, and in the direction of Mission Dolores. Perhaps not many years hence the whole shores of North Beach and South Beach, Mission Bay, and the Bay itself will be covered with streets and houses, quays and long piercing piers . . . . existing surveys . . . already exhibit these places, both on land and sea, divided and fairly mapped out into streets and wharves."[75]

Tichenor's Ways, 1864. *Not much more than a narrow shelf of pebbled beach with a few tool houses, but H. B. Tichenor made his fortune at Steamboat Point and sold this lot for a 1000% profit to the Central Pacific.*

THE SILVER ERA, 1860-1870

The Look of the Land—Long Bridge Spans the Bay

"This city is growing southward," reported the *Alta California* on May 2, 1864. "A year ago the waters of the southern bay dashed against a bleak and lonely front, stretching from a rocky barren and forlorn ridge, for a distance of half a mile or more. Since then, what a change! The foot of Third Street is now the terminus of the Omnibus Railway, and the hotel whose enterprising proprietor, Farr, has done so much for excavating that thoroughfare to bring cars to the bay waters, is reaping a rich reward for his exertions. Steamboat Point which was but four years ago almost uninhabited waste is now covered with manufactories, shops, saloons and dwellings. . . . on the foot of Third Street the Citizens Gas Company is engaged in an immense enterprise, which when fully carried out must involve an expenditure of one million dollars. This company's land is bounded by Townsend, Second and Berry. They have two lots of 275 feet. In the rear of this front is a precipitous bank of soft rock and dirt, presenting a face towards the bay of 100 feet in height. From this cliff the earth is obtained for filling up the water lots below. At the present, some 75 hands are employed in working into the cliff and carting the rock and dirt to the beach below. Laborers are industriously engaged in 'cribbing' the waterfront lots and filling in the bank . . . Nature has done much for this enterprise. The precipitous cliff overhanging the bay affords ample materials in way of stone and earth for filling the water lots whilst the shallowness of the waters permits the powerful steam engines to keep otherwise submerged lands dry."

Allowing for hyperbole, the *Alta's* description of the city's growth along the waterfront to the south is correct and useful. "Cribbing" consisted of constructing heavy, wooden, criss-crossed racks to hold rocks in place as the base for fill in the soft mud of Mission Bay. Sand and softer earth were then dumped on top of the rock-piled cribs, all in an effort to stem the tidal sweep.

Because Mission Bay was filled over a long period of time—from 1860 to as late as 1910—the material came from many sources. First leveled was the 100-foot sandhill on Townsend Street, then the steam paddy dumped sand and dirt taken from Fourth, Fifth and Sixth streets and from south of Market to the bay. The rock and dirt taken from the Second Street cut in 1869 was used. The serpentine rock from Irish Hill was blasted away and dumped into both Mission Bay and Islais Cove. From the 1870s to the 1890s there was continuous casual filling from garbage dumps along the line of Seventh and Eighth streets, near Berry. Finally, the earthquake rubble from 1906 completed the job, although watery puddles remained to be filled-in even later.

Long Bridge, 1867. *Muybridge made this view for the then-popular three-dimensional stereopticon viewers found in most Victorian parlors. The dramatic illusion of horsecar tracks meeting in the distance made the Potrero seem even further removed from the city than it was. Gallandett and Purdy's Half-Way House, with a star over the front door, is on the left. The larger, adjacent house in the foreground may be their home, as they are listed in the city directory as residing on Long Bridge. Dimly seen on the right are fences for the Mission Bay oyster beds belonging to the Morgan Oyster Company.*

Gray & Gifford's Birdseye View of San Francisco, 1868. *Diagrammatic view with keyed code may be found in notes.*

Smelt Fishing from Long Bridge, 1869. *The* South of Market Journal *recalled that Hobbs Wharf, off Long Bridge, "was a great place for Sunday and holiday fishing. If one did not get there at an early hour you hadn't a chance to drop your line. There were not many fancy fishing outfits seen then, mostly long bamboo poles. . . . There were booths along the wharf where you could rent one and buy your bait. Imagine hundreds of these poles projecting out, about a yard apart. The fish caught were smelt— hundreds of these silvery, graceful fighting fish."*[77]

Long Bridge—The most dramatic evidence of the city's southern expansion can be seen in the birdseye view of 1868—Long Bridge made the connection. Piles were driven for the bridge in February 1865, and the Potrero span was completed in 1867. Long Bridge followed the line of Fourth Street, where it made a nearly right-angle turn, spawned Hobbs Wharf reaching east into deep water, then continued across the shallow mudflats of Mission Bay to Kentucky Street, across the entrance to the Islais estuary and south towards Hunters Point. As can be seen in Gifford's highly accurate view, Long Bridge effectively enclosed three-fourths of Mission Bay. A drawbridge at Fourth Street enabled scow schooners and other shallow-drafted craft to enter Mission Bay, but only at high tide.

With the aid of the numbered key (in the notes[76]) it is possible to locate the Shot Tower on First Street, near the large square of the Oriental Warehouse, one of the few buildings shown here that is still intact. In the cove at the foot of Second Street is a full-rigged ship on Tichenor's marine railway. Nearby, the plume of smoke is from the new gasworks. The small bump outside Mission Bay is Mission Rock and the smokestack on Potrero Point is part of the Pacific Rolling Mills. The Rope Walk is seen to the south, with its 1,000-foot shed extending to a wharf with a small two-masted schooner alongside. In the far south is Hunters Point Drydock, and inland is the Bay View Racetrack—the effective end of the line for the Bay View Railroad that operated horsecars on the iron tracks on Long Bridge.

Constructed in anticipation of the expected business boom of the railroad, Long Bridge provided "rapid transit" for workmen from the city to the Potrero and Hunters Point, formerly reached only by boat or circuitous roads. On Sundays, Long Bridge became the focal point for south-of-Market fun. Smelt fishing from the long causeway was so popular that elbowroom was at a premium. The city's rowing clubs found the broad, sunny expanse of Mission Bay ideal for races and built their boathouses on pilings next to the bridge. There were boats for rent to row out to Mission Rock, and salt-water bathhouses built right out over the bay.

The recreational appeal of Long Bridge was not limited to the south-of-Market working class. The San Francisco Yacht Club's building was at the corner of Long Bridge and Steamboat Pier at the time that Henry B. Platt was commodore and W. H. Davis was secretary of the club. With the clubhouse at hand, yachtsmen moored their boats nearby, as can be seen in the Muybridge view of the *Emerald* (title page). The *Emerald*, an elegant sloop, won the San Francisco Yacht Club's first regatta. Next to the clubhouse, James Gallandett and G. W. Purdy opened a halfway house, confident that a day on the bay would raise many a thirst.

Small cafes and saloons perched on pilings next to the bridge where fishermen, Sunday sailors and families out for a stroll along sunny Mission Bay could stop for refreshment. Others rode the horsecars all the way to the end of the line to watch the horses run at Bay View. And there were the special Sunday excursions put on by the homestead associations, whose salesmen met the Bay View cars with their buggies and took families out on Hunters Point to inspect sites for future homes. A pleasant Sunday afternoon outing on Long Bridge had all the variety of sights, sounds, smells and activities that an urban park offers.

Real Estate Schemes: "Cut Down Rincon Hill and Fill In Mission Bay"

"The Silver Age was an intense, booming, hopeful decade . . . Few seem to understand that the decade between 1860 and 1870 was, next to the golden age of the '50s, the most important in the history of California. It was the period of transition from the fierce exploitation of the pioneers who looked only on the region as a thing to be despoiled of its treasures and abandoned. It saw valleys changed into broad oceans of waving grain. It saw the foothills crowned with

Rincon Hill Slips Into Oblivion.

The Latham mansion (above) was the $300,000 gift of Milton Latham to his bride and where they lived in fashionable splendor atop Rincon Hill. In 1869 the Second Street cut destroyed the integrity of the hill as handsome homes teetered on the brink of a sixty-foot ditch. By 1920 Rincon Hill had become a desolate slum fit only for use as the footing to the San Francisco Bay Bridge.

thrifty vineyards, saw the beginnings of systematic irrigation . . . saw a mighty foreign commerce develop, saw the treasures of the Comstock Lode unlocked, saw a railroad stretch from the Atlantic to the Pacific . . . everyone at last realized that gold was the smallest part of the state's resources and the outlook was as broad as the horizon of mid-ocean." So wrote Asbury Harpending from a comfortable old age in 1913, looking back at the most tumultuous decade of his own life—in which real-estate ventures played no small part.[78]

The treasure of the Comstock Lode was the major factor in what occurred. San Francisco had experienced a panic in 1855 when Harry Meiggs absconded, leaving a number of her citizens considerably worse off. The real-estate boom of 1853 leveled off and dropped as the supply of gold shipped from the mines appeared to have peaked. What had been overheated speculation cooled to something more normal, which by contrast seemed to be a depression.

With tremendous California-style luck, the discovery of the Comstock Lode of silver paid out $6 millon; by 1863, the figure had doubled. In 1864 Comstock silver reached $16 million; adding its value to the gold that year, $55 million in treasure passed through San Francisco. Money continued to pour into the city, generating heavy trading in mining stocks. Then, in 1874, the Big Bonanza struck, bringing in a million dollars a day for two months.[79]

Montgomery Street Straight—The heady prospect of San Francisco's peninsula becoming the terminus for the transcontinental railroad, coupled with the new flow of capital from the Comstock, injected new life into real-estate speculation, especially schemes affecting the southern waterfront. The rallying cry of real-estate promoters of the '60s was "Montgomery Street Straight!"

The possibility of connecting the financial district by a broad avenue directly to the Potrero and Mission Bay opened dizzy possibilities for promoting real estate. The idea was to extend Montgomery Street diagonally as a wide thoroughfare to the southern part of the city, joining Connecticut Street in the Potrero to the Montgomery Street financial district. Hittell reports: "This scheme was carried through the supervisors and passed over the mayor's veto; commissioners were appointed, and they made an elaborate report, with the estimate of the expense, but the engineer in laying off the map of the work, assumed incorrectly that the blocks intersected were exactly of the size proposed in the original survey. The consequence was that the lines of the new street were not straight, but showed a little offset like a saw-tooth at every crossing. This defeated the enterprise."[80] But another connection from the financial district to Steamboat Point had been brewing and came to a boil.

Middleton's Move—John Middleton, an auctioneer and real- estate broker, owned a lot at Second Street and Bryant. In 1863 Middleton proposed cutting through Rincon Hill on Second Street, then the fashionable center of San Francisco's best neighborhood. The idea was soundly put down on all sides, but Middleton persisted. He ran for the state legislature and was elected in 1868, whereupon he successfully devoted himself to getting his bill passed. San Francisco's Mayor Thomas H. Selby refused to carry out the order; his own fancy residence was on Rincon Hill at Harrison Street. The State Supreme Court ordered that the legislative act be carried out, and in 1869 the giant earth moving took place.

The original cost-estimate was $90,000 but the direct expense was $385,000. "The rock being non-cohesive, bulged downward and inward, like the filling of a swampy piece of land . . . the ground would sink . . . thereby endangering workmen by caving in."[81] As landslides endangered the houses that teetered on the edge of the muddy abyss, wealthy residents began to consider moving to the peninsula or to Oakland. Asbury Harpending looked at the problem and came up with a proposal.

Harpending's Plan—Of the Second Street cut, he wrote, "It was a sordid bit of real-estate roguery . . . but it was an accomplished fact. . . . The old high-priced residence property was going for a song. As the 'Hill' had ceased to be either beautiful or useful, Ralston and I calmly proposed to pull it down. We planned to have the city buy the property, which could be purchased for $12,000,000 . . . and grade it to the Market Street level. . . . Many million cubic yards of excavated material were to be used to fill in a 150-acre tract of tide-land offered to the city by the State at a nominal price, lying between the Pacific Mail docks and Islais Creek; also to reclaim China Basin [Mission Bay], at least, in part. The cost of grading and reclamation work was estimated at $7,500,000. . . . In other words, the city was asked to issue bonds for $12,000,000 and receive in payment over 200 blocks of choice property."[82]

Harpending was delegated by his partner, William Ralston, to persuade the state legislature to put through two bills. One bill advocated Harpending's proposal to extend his own New Montgomery Street all the way through to the bay. Harpending owned the Sutter Street gore (a triangular lot created by the diagonal line of Market Street), as well as other Market Street property. That same year he built the Harpending Block, between First and Second streets and the Grand Hotel, at the corner of Market and New Montgomery. The second bill allowed the city to acquire Rincon Hill, level it and fill-in the tidelands of Mission Bay.

Two "vote brokers" controlled the state legislature at that time, and Harpending "casually passed $35,000 at our first interview" to these political bosses. In addition, "I practically chartered a well-known restaurant in Sacramento and threw it open to my friends."[83] With some fancy footwork that included waylaying the governor's secretary on his way to the senate chambers bearing the governor's veto of these two bills, Harpending got what he and Ralston wanted.

Furious at Harpending's tactics, the governor refused to certify that the bills were law. Harpending took Governor Haight to court—and won.[84] It would seem that the fate of Rincon Hill and Mission Bay was settled in 1870. However, Harpending left for England to fleece the London stockmarket with western mining stocks and salt a diamond mine. Ralston was preoccupied with financial complications at the Comstock. Other parties (perhaps Milton Latham and John Parrott, who had earlier opposed the idea of an avenue cutting across their Rincon Hill front yards) put through a legislative bill that repealed the Harpending-Ralston plan for leveling Rincon Hill to fill in Mission Bay.

South Beach View of Mission Bay. In 1869 Joseph Lee, one of San Francisco's best marine artists, made this meticulous study standing on the Pacific Mail Dock, looking south from the foot of First Street. The railroad spur is on the bulkhead, built to start filling the land northwest of First and Townsend. A ship is hauled up on Tichenor's ways at the foot of Second Street, just in front of the newly completed Citizens' Gasworks. The smokestack marks the site of the Pacific Oil and Lead Works. This view of South Beach, the northeastern boundary of Mission Bay, was made as the building boom was just underway in anticipation of the completion of the transcontinental railroad. In the distance is Potrero Point; Long Bridge is concealed by the cluster of new industries at the foot of Second Street.

SOUTH WATERFRONT
INDUSTRIES OF THE 1880s

Building the Citizens' Gas Works, Spring 1865. *Cutting down the 100-foot sandhill on Townsend, between Second and Third streets, produced the fill for this new million-dollar enterprise. The two-story brick building faced the outer edge of Mission Bay so that it was possible for the ships from England, Wales and Australia to come alongside and dump their coal cargo.*

King Street runs between the new 115-foot gas holder and the gasworks. To the right, a wharf from Third Street nudges out into Mission Bay. Long Bridge, on its first leg to the Potrero, is only months completed, yet several small buildings have appeared; one is on Hobbs Wharf extension to deeper water where big four-masters could moor.

Stone Dry-Dock at Hunters Point. *The first industrial site at Hunters Point, built in 1868, the dry-dock had impressive dimensions: 465 feet long at the top, 400 feet long at the bottom, 120 feet wide at the top, narrowing to 60 feet wide at the bottom. The pumps threw out 40,000 gallons of water a minute and could empty the dock in 3.5 hours. This view, taken about 1870, shows the Pacific Mail Steamship Company's coastwise steamer, the sidewheeler* Montana, *in for repairs.*

Boatyards at Hunters Point, 1869. *Possibly a family outing to consider buying a lot on credit from the Haley-O'Neil Homestead Association at Hunters Point. Their view (near the corner of Keith and Evans streets) would take in the extension of Long Bridge in the background, boat-building yards and a marine railway, and small farms and workmen's quarters at the left. This may be the boatyard of William Munder, one of the first boat builders in this area whose specialty was scow schooners like the big one drawn up on the ways. Small boatyards such as this one persisted at Hunters Point right up through the 1920s. Carpenters, shipwrights and ship joiners specialized in building wooden boats here—everything from yachts such as those built by W. F. Stone, to three-masted lumber schooners. But these scattered yards were never big employers with the capacity to bring a booming prosperity to Hunters Point.*

Pacific Rolling Mills. *This first great ironworks on the south waterfront rolled its first bar of iron in July 1868. At the time Muybridge took this stereo view in 1869, the mills produced bar iron and had a capacity of 3,000 tons a year. Later they erected puddling furnaces and produced pig iron. From these mills came iron for the railroad; wrought-iron shafts for steamships and mills; I-beams for bridges, girders and housebuilding; rod, bar, and angle iron, chains, bolts and nuts; entire iron bridges; and the iron rails for streetcars and cable cars in San Francisco. By 1880, the mill ran day and night, producing 30,000 tons a year and employing 450 men at wages higher than on the East Coast. Irish immigrants headed for the big mills the moment they arrived in town; skilled iron moulders from Scotland made up a large part of the work crew.*

THE RAILROADS ARE COMING, 1860-1873

San Francisco's opinion of the transcontinental railroad was extremely ambivalent. On the one hand it was an article of faith that the city that became the terminus would enjoy prosperity unequalled. Only the solitary sobering prediction of Henry George was at odds.[86] On the other hand, San Francisco's geographic position as a deepwater port on the end of a peninsula presented a dilemma. Eager for the cornucopia of economic benefits the transcontinental connection would bring, and nervous that someone else might run off with the prize, it was considered crucial that San Francisco's monied interests should control railroad strategy and protect the city's future. But the most able proponent of the railroad to the Pacific was a man apparently more interested in solving the technical problems of accomplishing "the work of the age" than in his financial returns: Theodore Dehon Judah, an engineer for the Sacramento Valley Railroad—a man obsessed with a vision.

Although the Pacific Railroad Convention of September 1859 was held in San Francisco, with distinguished representatives on hand from every California county, as well as Washington and Oregon, it was Judah "who pondered the problem and took into his confidence a few businessmen in Sacramento and urged the formation of a company."[87]

Judah had scrambled up and down the passes of the Sierra Nevada, crossing the mountain range twenty-three times as he calculated again and again the difficult problems of building trestles around precipitous cliffs and across deep gorges, and tunneling into hard rock. So persuasive was "Crazy Judah," with his topographic profiles of the mountain passes and his sense of urgency, that in June 1861 several small-time entrepreneurs from Sacramento got together the funds to incorporate the Central Pacific Railroad.

On July 2, 1862, in the dark hours of the Civil War, President Lincoln signed the Pacific Railroad Act, pressured by the fear that the western states, led by California, might form an independent union. The act was the political plum of the age. Subsidies were to be generous: $16,000 per mile for track laid in flat country and $48,000 in the mountains, plus land grants to the railroad of 6,400 acres per mile, later amended upwards to 12,800 acres for every mile of track laid.

San Francisco reacted to the news with a tumultuous celebration. From Portsmouth Plaza 100 cannon fired; police, firemen and everyone else paraded—processions started early and hit every saloon in town, several times. When hangovers cleared and calm returned, a certain uneasiness took over that was reflected in the press. Lucius Beebe was probably correct when he later wrote, "What clouded the brow of San Franciscans, however, was the fact that when the great undertaking was finally inaugurated by breaking the ground in 1863, and the surveyors were driving stakes in the Sierra foothills, the moving spirits were not august representatives of Montgomery Street's monied circles but four all but unknown and completely unimportant businessmen from the pastoral reaches of Sacramento. Leland Stanford was a grocer; Charles Crocker a drygoods merchant; and Collis P. Huntington and his partner Mark Hopkins were dealers in hardware, vendors of fuses and blasting powder and wheelbarrows."[88] How had the most important technological marvel of the times happened to fall into the hands of amateurs in the art of marrying politics to money and coming up with power?

San Francisco newspapers simply could not grasp the magnitude of the situation. Calling it the "Dutch Flat Swindle," they downgraded the real implications of "the race of the age" to a smart move on the part of a few Sacramento

Central Pacific Cuts Through Blue Canyon. *Blasting their way through Sierra granite made the Central Pacific route move slowly, although urged on by stories of the Union Pacific's legendary John S. Casemont who carried a bull whip and got his crews to lay seven and three-quarters miles of track west of the Green River in a single day.*

businessmen to build a short-line railroad to Dutch Flat and siphon off the valuable freighting profits from the Comstock mines. San Francisco had been outmaneuvered and was now in the position of being only one of a gaggle of willing, would-be brides whose fate was up to a suitor who proved to be undependable and shrewd. The most substantial hope for linking San Francisco to Sacramento lay in the San Jose and San Francisco Railroad.

After three false beginnings in nine years, the San Jose and San Francisco Railroad got off to an organized start in 1860, financed by Peter Donahue's ironworks. The first plan, drawn up by William Lewis in 1851, called for constructing a bridge on pilings, running east of the San Bruno Mountains to cross Mission Bay into San Francisco, much the way Long Bridge was constructed fourteen years later. But tempted by county bond subsidies paid directly to the railroad, the new owners decided to route the line inland, where more voters stood to gain direct benefit and could be expected to be generous at the polls. The other attraction of the inland route became obvious in 1862, when "C.B. Polhemus, one of the directors of the railroad, had William Lewis plat the town of San Mateo at the point where the railroad right-of-way crossed San Mateo Creek."[89]

On February 16, 1864, the new line was complete, and in San Jose the railroad's president, Judge Timothy Dame, announced that the Central Pacific Railroad had given both the San Jose and San Francisco Railroad and the Western Pacific the right to construct the last link in its mighty transcontinental span. Thus it would appear that San Francisco had no reason to doubt its supremacy as the port meant to be the railroad terminus. But this was not the case, mostly because of murky doings in Oakland.

Horace Carpentier, a waterfront squatter in Oakland in 1852, wound up in March 1868 as the sole possessor of the Oakland waterfront. He proceeded to deed this waterfront property to a four-day-old corporation known as the Oakland Waterfront Company.[90] The next day, April 1, 1868, this just-born company conveyed to the Western Pacific Railroad 500 acres of Oakland tidelands. In return, the Western Pacific (now identical in management with the Central Pacific) agreed to construct a railroad to its waterfront land-grant in Oakland within 18 months, in exchange for half a million in gold coin, or else turn over its rights to the city of Oakland. Oakland citizens were inclined to "forgive the highly suspicious character" of this maneuver in their celebration at having won the terminal from their rival across the bay. San Franciscans were dismayed, and the events that followed reflect a sense of panic and a dark suspicion that their city was a pawn in the power of the "Big Four."

The Railroad Completed: Extravagant Hopes vs. Realized Results

"The driving of the last spike of the Central-Union Pacific Railroad, on the ninth of May, 1869, giving a continuous iron track from Sacramento to New York, was recognized and celebrated as one of the great events of the age, but to San Francisco it did not bring the anticipated benefits. Her citizens had calculated upon too much, and had invested their money on the basis not of realized results, but extravagant expectations, and when the completion of the road compelled a comparison between results and expectations, it was found that the prices of land generally, and especially in the suburban districts, were far beyond any permanent demand. Everybody wanted to sell, and nobody to buy; and a general and severe panic ensued. . . . The opening of the railroad between Sacramento and Oakland, by way of Stockton, in September [1869] made no perceptible improvement in the situation." So wrote J. S. Hittell in 1878, one of the most reliable observers of San Francisco's commercial history.[91]

At this ebb in San Francisco's hopes, the Big Four made another move to broaden their empire. The San Jose and San Francisco Railroad had extended its system to Gilroy and hoped to go over Pacheco Pass to the Colorado River

High Noon at Promontory, 1869. *Under the funnel-shaped smokestack of the Union Pacific's "Jupiter," their chief engineer, Grenville M. Dodge joined hands with the Central Pacific's chief engineer, Samuel S. Montague. The race was over as a double band of iron stretched across the United States. Champagne corks popped as the golden spike set off a telegraph connection across the nation—"The work of the age is complete."*

A.J. RUSSELL, OAKLAND MUSEUM

to connect with the new Atlantic and Pacific Railroad that was planned to head west from the Missouri. Peter Donahue enlisted the financial backing of San Francisco's most powerful banker, William Ralston. Together they incorporated the Southern Pacific Railroad. This move posed a real threat to the Central Pacific, whose management responded with $3.5 million and bought the San Francisco and San Jose Railroad and its planned Southern Pacific route.

The Central Pacific now turned to San Francisco and asked the city for a million-dollar subsidy to finance the railroad south of Gilroy, with the understanding that the terminus for this southern railroad line would be in Mission Bay. As attractive as this possibility was, San Franciscans went to the polls and defeated the bond issue, but narrowly. The *Daily Evening Bulletin* analyzed the returns: "This policy of coquetting with various towns, coaxing and threatening by turns, as if to get as much as possible from each, always holding in reserve an unavowed ulterior motive, is hardly the best one to win confidence."[92]

The next affront to San Francisco appeared in the form of a bill before Congress to deed Yerba Buena Island to the Western Pacific, from where the railroad would construct a causeway to Oakland and build warehouses and a terminal on the island. San Francisco saw this as giving away land to create another commercial city in the bay, a port to be designed and controlled by the railroads, who would then have their own wharves for shipping. Traditionally, Yerba Buena Island had been a military reservation, and federal engineers declined to go along with losing their island in the bay. They issued an opinion that such a connecting causeway would silt up the bay and diminish the tide. The outcry from San Francisco was so great that the bill was defeated in the Senate. But the idea of a railroad bridge across the bay persisted.

With the exception of the *Alta*, San Francisco newspapers mounted a campaign, with the nervous blessing of the business community, for a railroad bridge connection directly from Oakland to San Francisco. "If the reader will take into consideration that the bay is a sort of abyss that divides the great overland railroad from San Francisco, its western terminus, after it has traversed the country over 3,000 miles . . . he will comprehend at once the necessity for spanning this gap to deliver freight and passengers to the heart of the city." So wrote the editor of the *Call* on October 10, 1872.

The city fathers offered to build the railroad bridge as described at an estimated cost of $16 million; to build a harbor belt-line railway to connect all the city piers; and to fill-in the tidelands of Mission Bay to create land for right-of-way for the Central Pacific. Their only caveat was that *all railroads should have equal rights to use* this proposed facility. The Central Pacific countered with an offer to build the bridge and belt-line railroad themselves if San Francisco would come up with $2 million and give them the *sole right* to the land of Mission Bay. A compromise solution appeared to be at hand, but the Central Pacific further demanded the right to take the terminus away from San Francisco if business conditions warranted it. This was too much for Mayor W. Alvord, who vetoed the supervisors' recommendations, and the idea of a railroad bridge died.

But if San Francisco never became the land terminus for the transcontinental railroad, the Southern Pacific and Santa Fe Mission Bay freight terminals shaped the character of business in the south part of the city. The north waterfront warehouse district, built to serve the clippers of the 1860s and 70s, was largely relocated after 1906 to the southern part of the city where Mission Bay's important network of railroad tracks, warehouse complexes, and roundhouses also connected to the Beltline Railway leading to every wharf in the city. Unique in North America, this harbor railroad connected ships to trains after 1896 in a totally efficient cargo handling operation. Southern Pacific's Third and Townsend passenger depot handled a busy commuter business with comfort, speed, and efficiency remembered with nostalgia by today's freeway victims.

The San Francisco Terminus of the Central Pacific Railroad in 1878. *This was the new Ferry Building, completed in 1875. In addition to transcontinental passengers, thousands of workers commuted to San Francisco. From 1873 to 1877 the number of passengers increased from 2,655,671 to 5,570,555.*

FRANK LESLIE'S ILLUSTRATED NEWSPAPER, 1878

MISSION BAY TIDELANDS CONTROVERSY, 1868-1879

The most important legislative act that determined the future of Mission Bay was California's Tidelands Act of 1868. Various bills were introduced, amended, debated and commented upon in editorials headed: "Tidelands Conspiracy," "Behemoth Tidelands Bill," "Tidelands Grab." From this historical distance it is impossible to know what kind of secret alliances were formed to push through various bills. The homestead associations were suspected of being front organizations for the railroads. Whereas initially the railroads could do no wrong, the monopolistic practices of the Central Pacific in action set up a strong counter-reaction that reached a fever pitch in San Francisco and put Governor Haight in office in 1867. Here was a governor who at least spoke against such methods, even though his own actions proved to have less integrity than his stated convictions.

Rumors and the Press—Since the thrust of various tidelands bills was to survey the tidelands of Mission Bay and Hunters Point and set aside railroad grants for rights-of-way, the San Francisco press assumed that the legislation was entirely aimed at giving the south waterfront to the Central Pacific. Among the typical stories is one picked up by the *San Francisco Bulletin* from the Sacramento *Union*, in early March 1868: "Those who are acquainted with the tendency of growth and business of San Francisco know that it is in the direction of the localities included in the proposed railroad grant . . . Real estate values are more rapidly increasing in the direction of Mission Bay and South San Francisco than anywhere else . . . It is hardly extravagant to expect that in less than ten years hence the heaviest shipping and wholesale business will be in the region of Long Bridge and Mission Bay . . . The property asked in this bill . . . includes the whole of Mission Bay and hundreds of acres further out than the mouth of the bay in the deep water of San Francisco Bay. . . . The whole grant asked to extend the waterline a mile and a half south of Hunters Point. . . . Central Pacific Railroad Company and their partners of the shadowy title would realize many millions, while the State would get perhaps $200,000 . . . It would be an outrage to pass this bill."[94]

Early in March, 1868, a *San Francisco Bulletin* editorial appeared, entitled "The Tideland Conspiracy," which said in part: ". . . all rival claimants . . . have united in support of the bill which proposes to give the railroad companies all the southern frontage of this city. The most prominent parties in this combination are the Central, Western, and Southern Pacific and San Jose Railroad Companies, whose interests are now identical; the South San Francisco Dock and Wharf Company, which already owns one or two miles of water frontage, which the Legislature is asked to extend to deep water; the association which holds certificates to 1,500 acres of land in Mission Bay . . . and finally Carpentier, who owns the Oakland frontage, with his railroad and real estate associates. These parties are all represented at Sacramento by influential men who have capital at command . . . further backed by a powerful professional lobby, embracing a number of notorious politicians and schemers."[95]

The Tidelands Bill, as passed March 30, 1868—The daily revelations of the press, combined with the truly astonishing land grabs proposed in the various tidelands bills introduced in the legislature, served to modify the final product. The railroads wound up with 150 acres, mostly in Mission Bay, or the equivalent of 345.5 fifty-vara lots. With the streets and three market places included, another 42 acres were added for a grand total of 192 acres or 442 fifty-vara lots. However, these streets and three squares that were set aside as market places "reserved

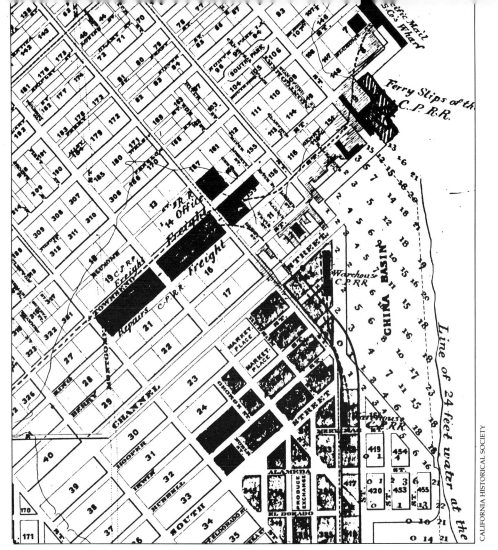

Mission Bay Railroad Land. This hand-colored manuscript map is the official 1870 Map of the City & County of San Francisco, drawn to show the extent of lands donated to the railroads (lighter wash) by the state, lands purchased by the railroads (darker wash) and land leased to the railroads (shown as cross-hatched) at the foot of Second Street, formerly Tichenor's Ways. The railroad right-of-way extended south over Hunters Point and included donated land in Islais Creek Basin. Also off this portion of the map, by reason of scale, are lands purchased by the railroad on the banks of Mission Creek. The map inset notes: "60 acres were donated, 58 acres were purchased, 4 were leased, for a total of 122 acres, plus 28 acres of tide lands donated for right of way for a total of 150 acres." And further, "If the streets and the three Market Places lying within the 60 acre donation be granted to the R.R. Co. it will add about 42 acres to the above, making the Grand Total 192 acres or equivalent to 442 fifty-vara lots."

for public use" were specifically withheld from the grant. The accompanying 1870 map gives a clear idea of the lands involved.

The "Act to survey and dispose of certain salt marsh and tidelands belonging to the State of California" ordered the governor to appoint a Board of Tidelands Commissioners to "take possession of all the salt marsh and tidelands lying under water . . . belonging to the State of California . . . surveyed to a point not beyond twenty-four feet of water at the lowest stage of the tide. . . ." All such real property to be mapped and sold at public auction. Streets, docks and piers, canals and drains were reserved to the city of San Francisco.

The Southern Pacific and Western Pacific railroads were granted 30 acres each, exclusive of streets, basins and public squares, on land south of Channel Street and outside the redline waterfront of Mission Bay.[96] In addition the railroads were given a right-of-way not to exceed 200 feet in width. In return the railroads had to agree to spend $100,000 within thirty months to construct a San Francisco terminus. After the time was extended in 1872, the Mission Bay railroad terminus was completed.

The Tideland Commissioners were to have the power to settle claimants' disputes over water lots and to sell the tidelands as mapped and surveyed. All public monies were conveyed by the commissioners to the state. The three-man Tidelands Board appointed by Governor Haight was a powerful body, and it could be said to the commissioners' credit that there was little criticism of their mode of operation, carried out as it was under the spotlight of every newspaper in San Francisco. They were to be involved in endless hearings of rival claims, sometimes stacked five deep on a single lot.

Trouble on Mission Creek: Squatters Riot

What was to prove one of the more troublesome sections of the 1868 Tidelands

Act stated, "Where any settler was on the first day of January, A.D. 1868 in bona fide actual possession of any one lot by himself or tenant, and any additional lot in which he shall have had substantial improvements at the time aforesaid . . . may purchase such lot . . ." prior to public auctions, in effect, at private hearings before the Tidelands Commission.[97] As can well be imagined, Mission Bay squatters (who preferred to be called "settlers") interpreted the phrase "substantial improvements" as being fine-tuned to their own interests, since many of them were living in houses on the banks of Mission Creek and on filled portions of Mission Bay. "Bona fide actual possession" was seen as an endorsement of the principle of "squatters' rights," an idea long cherished in the Potrero and Mission Bay.

One cloud that hung over Mission Bay–Potrero lands was the long and exhausting legal efforts by Mexican claimants, in this case the de Haros, to clear their titles through the courts. In 1867 the de Haro claim to more than 2,000 acres near the mission was rejected, as the courts ruled that the Mexican government had given the de Haros grazing rights but no clear title. On May 15, 1867 the *Alta* described the popular reaction: "At 7 o'clock a detachment of California Guard with two pieces crossed Long Bridge . . . they fired two hundred guns in honor of the settlers' victory. There was another gun in the vicinity of North's shipyard which also thundered forth a tremendous salute. . . . Early in the morning a mammoth bonfire was kindled on the highest point on Potrero Ridge . . . An impromptu meeting was held by the settlers . . . residents of the Potrero could breathe freely, now that this long contested controversy is settled . . ."

But having the major Mexican claim laid to rest by the Yankee courts gave all the more importance to the Tidelands Bill statement regarding "bona fide actual possession," which was taken to mean "being there." Rival claimants, some with titles going back to 1846, others to 1851 (with the sale of the Peter Smith water lots), moved into Mission Creek with pile drivers and a scow schooner armed with cannon (quickly dubbed the "Mission Creek Gunboat"); using pistols and knives they fought it out for possession.

On November 19, 1868, the *Alta* noted, "It will be remembered by our readers that within the past year Mr. Charles P. Duane shot Mr. Ross on Merchant Street for an alleged interference in this matter of title to lands. Yesterday morning, about 3 o'clock, several men made their appearance upon the ground and demanded possession. During the skirmish a man named Baxter was seriously wounded." And again, a week later, "The trouble on Mission Creek continues . . . the police have charge of the pile driver, mud-scow, or 'gunboat,' and they have instructions to allow no one on board . . . if parties owning the gunboat make any attempt to move it, and if those who ran the pile-driver on disputed territory attempted to use it, riotous proceedings would follow . . "

Some sixty men fought it out on Mission Bay's Block 40. Several were seriously wounded; that no one was killed was probably a matter of luck rather than restraint. Block 40 (seen below on the Tidelands Auction Map at the end of Channel Street, under the "Y" in Bay) lay between Berry and Channel streets and Seventh and Eighth streets. The block as shown in 1869 is partially in the salt marsh and partially under the waters of Mission Bay.

By 1876 the State Senate had appointed the Mission Creek Investigating Committee to look into disputed tidelands decisions. In one such case, the commissioners gave Duane title to more than two and a half blocks of land "that should have been sold at public auction for the benefit of the state," according to the *San Francisco Bulletin* on January 19, 1876. Duane, in fencing his tract, included his house on the upland that adjoins his tideland water lots. The *Bulletin* contended that the commissioners had no jurisdiction on the dry land portion of Duane's land and the fence on the tidelands portion was not sufficient improvement. "Duane was not the only one who obtained valuable salt marsh and

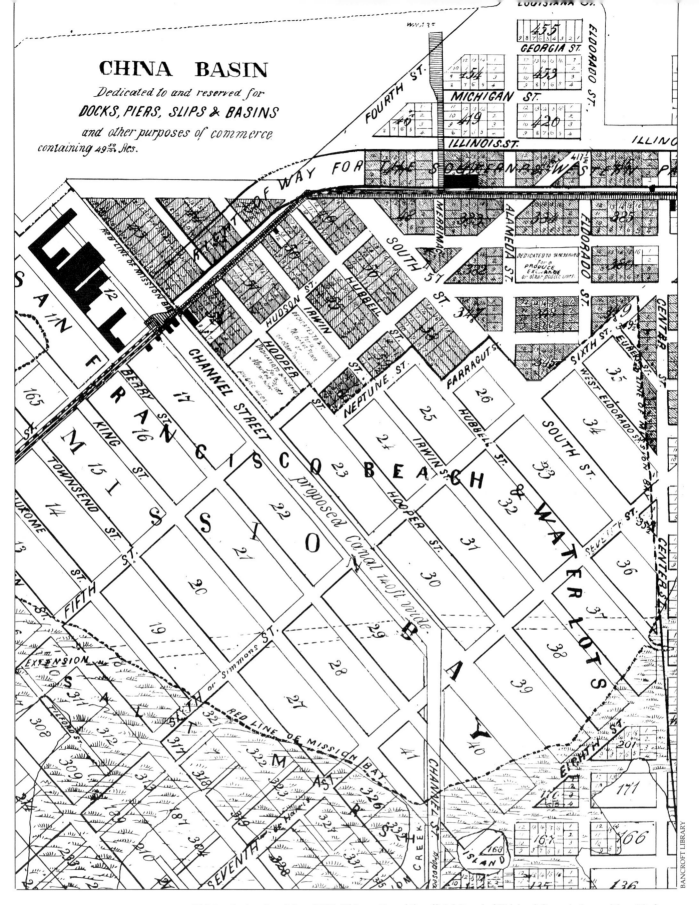

Tidelands Auction Map, 1869. *This portion of the official Board of Tideland Commissioners Map #3 shows some of the water lots to be auctioned in November 1869. The map is interesting because it shows a proposal to continue Channel Street's canal to Seventh Street at a width of 140 feet, then to angle and narrow it to meet the mouth of Mission Creek at a width of 60 feet. The irregular line of salt marshes is the "Red Line of Mission Bay." Inside the "Red Line" are water lots that were sold during the Peter Smith sales of 1853. The confusion over these various boundaries led to legal battles.*

tidelands by virtue of a house built on high ground. How about Ellis himself? Let the investigation at Sacramento be thorough."[98]

"The Ellis Land Grab Case" was fought in the 4th District Court in January 1877, as well as on the muddy banks of Mission Creek. Duane's land and many more blocks were involved in a far more expansive scheme. Part of the problem stemmed from the lack of precise definition of the boundaries of the original San Francisco Pueblo Grant. Ellis found it useful to claim that the winding line of Mission Creek was the pueblo boundary and the Tidelands Commissioners had agreed, considering the overflow lands to be within their jurisdiction. Thus they gave Ellis clear title to land he claimed to have owned since 1853. Ellis now enlarged his claim to include "all land on either side of Mission Creek, from Nineteenth Street to Channel Street and including the overflow land adjacent to the creek, property valued at something like $4,000,000. There are several hundred claimants who are defendants in this section."[99]

The Ellis claim was denied by the U.S. Circuit Court on July 29, 1878, when it rendered a decision that the pueblo lands of four square leagues (granted to Yerba Buena and confirmed to San Francisco on May 18, 1865) included the swamp land, "that is, the eastern boundary of the city follows the line of the ordinary high water, *crossing the mouths of streams*, and not following their banks."[100]

In another case, *Tripp* vs. *Spring*, Judge Field made a statement that had far-reaching consequences to the property holders in Mission Bay and the Potrero, when some twenty-two entire blocks were under disputed title: "Mission Creek never constituted any portion of the Bay of San Francisco any more than the Sacramento River constitutes a portion of the Bay of Suisun, or the Hudson River a portion of the Bay of New York . . . The boundary of the tract [confirmed to the city as part of the pueblo] runs along the Bay on the line of ordinary high water mark, as that existed in 1846, crossing the mouth of creeks running into the Bay, and that of Mission Creek, among others. The boundary would have been a singular one had it followed the windings of that creek and its branches, wherever the tide-waters of the Bay may have flowed."[101]

Judge Field's opinion had the further salutory effect of giving the settlers in the Potrero and Mission Bay what they had wanted, peace from further challenges of any real importance to their presence.

What the Tidelands Commissioners Disposed of, from 1868 to 1872—In carrying out the vast tidelands survey as ordered by the 1868 legislative act, the commissioners reported that 65,200 acres were surveyed, of which 13,200 were judged to be covered by state patents and legislative grants and therefore were not subject to sale. Of the remaining acres, 33,200 were reserved for canals and other aids to commerce and 14,400 were sold, as instructed, leaving only 4,400 surveyed acres unsold. The balance included the land between Black Point and Fort Point in San Francisco.[102]

Already concern was being expressed about filling-in the great bay of San Francisco, as evidenced by a letter to the *Chronicle* dated January 30, 1874: "In the course of an interview with Col. Mendell, U.S. Engineer, that gentleman showed me a map of the Bay of San Franciso which indicated that the State had parted with her title to the tidelands to an extent that there was absolutely nothing left to save . . . the water area in San Francisco Bay is in round figures 400 square miles, while the land covered by water has passed into private ownership to the extent of more than 300 square miles. If it were lawful to fill in all this submerged land, the harbor of San Francisco would be utterly destroyed."

In 1872, "Save the Bay!" had not yet been sounded—it would be another 100 years before reality set in and the importance of retaining salt marshes and wetlands reversed the seemingly immutable conception of "development seen as progress."

Largest of three small peaks on a submerged ridge, Mission Rock rose twenty-five feet above the bay waters and served as a navigational guide for ships. By 1884 it was more useful as an extended wharf to hold warehouses, as seen in the inset drawing made in 1900. H. B. Tichenor had his eye on Mission Rock when he sold out his marine railway to the railroad interests in 1870. He secured a tidelands' grant to some submerged land around the rock and built a drydock, expanding less than a fourth of an acre into four acres.

Filling In Mission Bay . . . 1884

The Coast Survey Map of 1884 demonstrates how Long Bridge became the focal point for filling in Mission Bay. Jutting out the line of Fourth Street, carrying the railroad lines to the Southern Pacific freight sheds between Townsend and King streets, Long Bridge by then had a man-made delta at Third Street.

The "busiest part of the port" in the late 1880s and '90s centered around Channel Street, with its finger piers reaching out to the scows and schooners bringing in bricks and cement, shingles and spars, lumber to be milled on Berry Street, grain for the South End Warehouse and hay for the horses that kept the city moving. Just north of the Channel Street entrance to the bay, steamers of the Pacific Mail Steamship Company arrived from New York and the Far East. At the foot of Second Street, Tichenor's Ways has been sold to the Southern Pacific for $250,000 and is now the pier where the big railroad ferryboat, the *Thoroughfare*, brings locomotives and freight cars to run along the King Street rails to the Southern Pacific freight yards.

The north side of Channel Street is very nearly filled in from Third to Sixth, where the map shows a slender finger of fill reaching south to connect with the line of Sixteenth Street, near the Point of Rocks. South of Berry, between Sixth and Seventh streets, an informal garbage dump persisted from 1878 until 1895, gradually extending until it covered twenty acres south of the channel. Garbage from the densely populated south-of-Market district came here at the rate of three hundred wagons a day. Before it was shoveled into the bay water, the "dump trust" sorted through everything for salvage. "With a general air of dejected doggedness, many were busily engaged with pitchfork, shovel or stick, sifting each load as it was dumped from the reeking, overflowing carts. Rags, old bottles, scraps of iron, old sacks, bricks, oystershells, half-decayed fruit and vegetables—all were prized.[103] Although the police sporadically raided "Dumpville," burning the shacks that were put on "railroad lands," the scavengers returned and business continued, since there were no neighbors to complain. The degree of pollution at Channel Street and in Mission Bay became so great that the water was sickening to smell and deadly to fall into.

On the 1884 Coast Survey Map, all that remains from Mission Creek's original estuary (as shown in 1852) is an inlet that hooks around toward Brannan and Eighth streets. By 1874, Mission Creek above Ninth and Brannan had been officially abandoned as a navigable stream.[104] All of the land east of Mission Creek's tidal remnant (south of Brannan and east to Fourth Street) had been progressively created by filling or spanning the waters of Mission Bay. The salt marsh at the southwestern edge of Mission Bay is more fenced than filled; only a few isolated farms appear on the 1884 chart.

Potrero Point—In contrast to the nearly empty edge of the old salt marsh is the industrial buildup at Potrero Point. Here the dream of the 1860s is realized by 1884. The Union Iron Works opened in 1882, directly adjoining the Pacific Rolling Mills, the point's first major manufacturing industry, dating back to 1866. The Western Sugar Refinery dominated the southern waterfront of Potrero Point. Within a few years, the Atlas Iron Works would locate here.

In spite of the depression, the big mills reverberated day and night, producing mining machinery, pumps, boilers, iron for the railroads, streetcar rails, bridges, marine hardware and big walking-beam engines, iron-clad monitors and cruisers for the Navy. Potrero production was the center of San Francisco's industrial output from 1884 through the first World War.

San Francisco paid higher wages to skilled craftsmen and industrial workers than could be earned in the East. But jobs were scarce and fought over. Poverty in the city was grinding and seemed never to end, bringing ugly outbreaks of anti-Chinese feeling as both races scrambled for any available work.

The men who worked on Potrero Point lived there as well. Bill Carr, sheriff's deputy in South San Francisco for forty-six years, came to Irish Hill as an infant in 1877 and grew up in the streets seen in the view below. The accompanying caption is his recollection.

"It was mostly all hotels . . . The Green House, run by Mike Farrell. The White House run by Hans Rasmussen. Cash's Hotel, run by Jimmy Cole. The San Quentin House run by Jim Gately. Gately took in the parolees from San Quentin and got them jobs in the rollin' mills . . . There was Paddy Kearns' Hotel, and outside the gashouse was Mike Boyle's steam beer dump . . . The boys from one hotel would challenge the boys from another and fight all Saturday afternoon in a hayrope ring outside Gately's Hotel. Then we'd all go in and knock off steam beers for a nickel a piece . . . You went up on Irish Hill when you got off work and you never left it until morning. Below it was Dutchman's Flat, where the Dutchmen from the old country lived. . . .Eight or nine hundred people use to live there . . . There were 98 wooden steps up the hill."[105] This view, taken in the 1890s, shows what was left of the serpentine hill, much of it having been blasted away and dumped in the bay.

WORK ON LAND AND WATER, 1880-1920

(Above) Channel Street, *looking toward the city, from Fourth to Third Streets, ca. 1885*

In the 1880s Channel Street had deep finger-piers that extended from the back doors of Berry Street wood-finishing businesses out to meet the incoming lumber schooners and scows loaded with hay, firewood, shingles and bricks. The south side of Channel Street, from Fourth to Third, was an open wharf for lumber. The photographer has set his tripod on the southern wharf to make this three-part panorama. Among the points of interest in this early view, *(1)* marks the line of Fourth Street, just before Long Bridge, and the two-story warehouse of the Sierra Lumber Company, which specializes in sugar pine and yellow pine. At the next small wharf *(2)* is the Patent Brick Company, and stacks of lumber can be seen at the San Francisco Lumber Company *(3)*.

The handsome brick warehouse *(4)* of the South Point Warehouse Company appears on the 1869 Coast Survey Map. In this view, sacks of grain lie just beyond the two scow schooners that are moored side by side. The tallest building on the skyline *(5)* is the Southern Pacific's Main Office at Fourth and Townsend. Ritch Street *(6)* is a small alleyway off King. The scow schooner stacked high with firewood *(7)* is at James Alexander's Wood Wharf. The big gas tank *(8)* is at the Pacific Gas Improvement Company, between King and Townsend streets, almost adjoining the Pacific Oil and Lead Works on King Street *(9)*. The Sacramento Brick Wharf *(10)* is loaded with pallets of brick. Drawn up at the foot of this wharf is yet another scow schooner, one of the workboats of the bay, flat-bottomed and, relative to its own size, capable of carrying an enormous load of bulk cargo. A diminutive launch, the kind that escorted sailing ships up the channel, noses up beside the scow. From earlier times, is the peaked roof of the South End Boat Club *(11)*, the focus of rowing on Mission Bay in the 1880s. The large gas tank *(12)* is on Second Street, between King and Townsend.

Lumber Was the Cash Crop. *The big four-masted schooner* Okanogan *discharges lumber at the Pope & Talbot lumberyard at Third and Berry. Their wharf was on Channel Street. By the time of the* Okanogan, *timber was coming from the Pacific Northwest in these big four-masters. Like most of the bigger lumber companies, Pope & Talbot owned a fleet of lumber schooners to carry the rough-milled lumber to their Channel and Berry street yards for finishing or sale.*

NAT'L MARITIME MUSEUM, S.F.

Sparmakers on Mission Creek. *Shaping spars with broadaxe and adze started with a taste for geometry and ended with a feel for finish. A skilled man at C. A. Castner & Co., dressing down a 100-foot mast, might bring to mind the unlikely image of a sculptor smoothing his work with a ten-pound razor. The mast in the foreground is about right for a scow schooner; the one in the background looks to be about as big as they came from the Northwest woods. This view of the sparmaker's crew, knee-deep in chips, is dated 1896—the craft is far older.*

NAT'L MARITIME MUSEUM, S.F.

Telfer & White's Berry Street Planing Mill. *Berry Street craftsmen produced the fancy woodwork trim and brackets for San Francisco homes. These men in derby hats probably frequented the nearby Cuckoo Nest. There were saloons at every corner, and midblock too, along Berry and Channel streets, which institutionalized the famous San Francisco "free lunch." The "schooner" of steam beer, going for a nickel, included an immense free spread of pickles, hard-boiled eggs, corned beef, sausages, hard rolls and cheese. Lunch at the corner saloon was a chance to exchange political views, which often led to explosive fist fights that caused the combatants to be escorted into the streets while wagers were laid all around as to how it would turn out.*[106]

At Boole and Beaton's Shipyard on Channel Street. *Fifty-six men stopped work on the big wooden collier (coal-carrying steamer) Ajax long enough to pose for the only photograph to come to light so far showing shipbuilding on Mission Creek. This view, donated by George San Faucon of the San Francisco Caulker's Union, was made in 1888. Mr. Beaton is number 19, Mr. Boole was elsewhere.*

Shipbuilding on the Channel 1880-1890s

Given the crowded berthing conditions on the channel after 1880, it is astonishing to see the size of the ships turned out by Alexander Hay, Matthew Turner and Boole and Beaton's yards at the head of Mission Creek. The Boole and Beaton crew (shown above) built *Tillamook, Cleone, Cosmopolis, Newsboy, Del Norte, Silver Springs, Westport, Rival* and *Ajax* (whose hull appears behind the gang).

Boole and Beaton's yard directly adjoined one of Alexander Hay's two yards, the one between Sixth and Seventh streets. During 1887 and 1888 Hay produced the steam schooners *Alcazar, Navarro, Point Arena, Pasadena, Noyo, Hooper, Point Loma, Venture, Scotia, Farallon, National City, Mendocino* and *Jewel.*[107]

These two builders were the largest constructors of steam schooners on the Pacific Coast at the time—and theirs were the vessels that revolutionized the lumber trade. With their ability to deliver on contract schedule, the steam-powered lumber vessels (there was not much "schooner" about them) could be relied on winter and summer to provide the inventories builders needed. The volume of lumber carried in a year by the twenty-three vessels launched by Hay and by Boole in 1887 and 1888 was as great as an armada of sailing ships might transport.

A news clipping from 1887 headlined: "MORE SHIPBUILDING—FOUR NEW VESSELS BEING CONSTRUCTED AT THE YARDS—BUSY SAW AND HAMMER Establishing a New Shipyard at the Foot of Fifth," describes Alexander Hay's shipyards on the channel: "A busy scene presents itself at the Sixth Street shipyards, where four large steam schooners are being constructed, and where one, launched on Thursday, is receiving the finishing touches. At the shipyard of Alexander Hay the steamer *Pasadena* is well under way and will be ready for launching about the first of next month. In length she is 150 feet over all, has a breadth of beam of 32 feet and 10 feet hold. Her carrying capacity is 400,000 feet of lumber. She is constructed of Oregon pine, with stem, stern and rudder posts of eastern Oak. Her fastenings are composed of galvanized iron and locust trunnels. She is being built for Kirkoff & Kuzner of Los Angeles, who will place her in the lumber trade between the latter city and Eureka, Humboldt Bay. Her cost is $45,000."[108]

After the turn of the century, the Channel Street shipbuilders moved south to Hunters Point or across the bay to Alameda and Oakland. Steam schooners began to be built increasingly closer to the source of the timber that made up their central cargo. Only a dozen steam schooners were completed in California yards after 1907, while 47 were built on the northwestern Pacific Coast.

Matthew Turner. *Probably the most experienced shipbuilder in North America in this period, Matthew Turner built 228 vessels. In addition to brigantines, barkentines and steamers, Turner completed 133 two-masted schooners, more than 60 for foreign owners.*

(*Above left*) John D. Spreckels. *A handsome brigantine of 267 tons, was launched at the head of Mission Creek in 1880. She was built by Matthew Turner for J. D. Spreckels' Hawaiian sugar trade. Like most of the vessels in that run, she carried passengers and was heavily rigged, including topmast stunsails which can be seen extended like giant wings in this picture.*

(*Above right*) Tahiti. *Another brigantine built by Matthew Turner on Mission Creek was the Tahiti, a brig of 190 tons gross burden, launched in 1881. The handsome Tahiti fell into evil hands in 1891 when Captain W.H. Ferguson used her for "blackbirding"—recruiting coffee plantation labor by legal and illegal means. She was found bottom up near Manzanillo "with no sign of life, nor were any bodies seen floating around."[109] Matthew Turner (seen in the inset) blamed the captain for not keeping her water casks filled.*

Jewel. *The steam schooner Jewel, built by Alexander Hay on Mission Creek, steams past Alcatraz with a load of lumber probably from the Mendocino Coast. She has a counter stern similar to that of the sailing schooners, and carries a small square foresail, a gaff foresail, and a leg-of-mutton mainsail. The fore-and-aft sails might steady her as she "beat" up the redwood coast under steam, and the square canvas could give her compound engine a boost as she ran before the northwest winds back to San Francisco.*

The Hay Wharf on Channel
Street. *"The hay dealers make a
warehouse of wharves, landing
their hay and keeping it there until
it is peddled off,"* complained the
San Francisco Call *in 1876. As
necessary as it was to feed the
thousands of horses that ran the
city's transport, the hay trade was
considered an unsightly, messy
fire hazard. San Francisco's Board
of Supervisors had promised the
China Basin (Mission Bay) area to
the harbor commission for the hay
dealers but had reneged in 1876.
By 1884 the haymen had their own
wharf, on the north side of the
channel, between Second and
Third streets, jutting off from
Pope & Talbot's lumberyard,
affording only a narrow passage
for scow schooners. Channel Street
became the focal point of an
enormous hay trade; often a dozen
or more scows could be seen here at
once, tied two or three abreast,
loaded with five or six tiers
of hay bales.*

Hay-Day on Channel Street, 1880-1920

Captain Fred Klebingat, served as a "donkeyman,"[110] when he arrived on the
south waterfront in 1909 at the age of twenty. The text that follows is from his
vivid recollections of Channel Street.[111] "At the end of Third Street there was a
narrow waterway, officially named Mission Creek, but I never heard it called
by such a refined title. It was an open sewer, a cesspool that emitted offensive
odors, especially at low water. Great bubbles of gas broke the surface. Here was
a creek the consistency of mud; the flow of the tides did not materially affect it.
We *knew* what the contents of the creek were! They said that if you fall overboard
you'll not last more than two minutes. They said if you took two gulps of that
stuff it would be the end of you. It would turn white lead paint black in one night.

"As bad as the stench was, still this was the busiest place on the San Francisco
waterfront. From Pope & Talbot's Lumberyard on the north side of the entrance,
and the Hay Wharf (opposite Pope & Talbot's) steam schooners, sailing vessels
and hay scows lined either side of the Creek, leaving barely enough space for
vessels to be towed down the middle. A couple of drawbridges spanned the
malodorous stream.

"Ships' crews groaned at the order that brought their vessels here—the escap-
ing gases from the creek discolored the paint of the hull inside and out. But
ships came to Shit Creek in droves to discharge their lumber cargoes and bay
scows came to the hay wharf to get rid of their hay deckloads.

"Men would get hungry and thirsty, even in these smelly surroundings, so
several saloons and cheap restaurants were at the foot of Third Street, near the
drawbridge that spanned the Creek."

Annie L. *Here the* Annie L., *built in 1900 by Emil Munder, at sixty-five feet long and measuring about 60 tons, brings in more than 350 bales of hay for San Francisco's horses. Hayloads were collected from as far afield as Sacrameento and Milpitas and at many points along the shallow creeks and sloughs between. There the shallow draft of a scow schooner such as the* Annie L. *could slide over the mud with the help of the tide, in areas closed to other types of watercraft.*

As vital as the hay trade was to the economy of the 19th century, hay dealers were not welcome at the wharves. During a single week in 1896, three fires started at the hay wharf were blamed on the careless manner in which scow men knocked out their pipes. Sometimes the fires spread to the scows alongside the wharf. If the mooring burned through and there was an ebb tide, a scow might drift out into the bay, burning picturesquely.[112]

Scow Schooner Reflections. *When the wind had failed, getting into Mission Creek required a "Swedish towboat" (the yawl boat carried by the scow) to pull her up those last few hundred feet to the wharf. If you look closely you can see that the steering wheel of the scow has been raised eight or nine feet so that the helmsman who has left his wheel and is standing on the top of his load, can see over the hay.*

"... Busiest Part of the Waterfront ..."

Klebingat remembers—"It was Pope & Talbot's lumber yard that we mostly visited; one thing was sure, more schooners and barkentines discharged here than in any other part of the creek. There might be a remote chance that we would meet a mate in a hurry to hire a man willing to work. Or we might meet a friend or former shipmate who was lucky and had a berth on one of these ships who might oblige us with a dollar or two.

"We watched the unloading for a while—the loads landed with the swinging gaff, tallymen standing about, a tallybook open in their left hand, noting each piece of lumber as it was removed from beneath the gear. Front men then piled the different sizes of lumber on two-wheeled carts, large clumsy affairs fitted with iron wheels. A cart is loaded, a teamster and his horse drop by. He flings a light chain over the load and cart on its high end . . . and connects it with the towing gear of his horse. They are off with the cart, its lower end dragging on the wharf, bound to a certain lumber pile where the load is stacked.

"It really never surprised us when no job was available. . . . It was one more case of—not what you knew, but WHO you knew. . . .

"Leaving Pope and Talbot we headed out the finger pier that angled out into the channel to accommodate the bay scows or scow schooners unloading hay. The scow schooners were made fast, sometimes three abreast, the inner one busy discharging its cargo . . . Several bay scows were now discharged and ready for another voyage. They moved to the outer tier, set their lowers, put down the center board, let go (some shoving off with the pike pole) and with a rubbing of strakes against their sisters they gathered headway . . . It took pure seamanship and good judgement to tack in this confined space."

Lumber Was Big Business. *A brigantine and a schooner (below left) discharge lumber by hand into carts in 1897, at a yard above the Fourth Street Bridge. By contrast, in the 1920s photograph (below right), a steam schooner unloads with the help of a steam winch. For immediate overland shipment, her cargo is restacked in the waiting railroad freight car pulled directly alongside on a spur track. The China Basin Building across the creek was built as part of the Del Monte Cannery empire in 1925.*

The Bascule Bridge Makes Way for Hay . . . *the* Nellie Rich *stops traffic as she passes under the Third Street drawbridge with a cargo of hay to unload in the upper channel.*

Steaming Down the Creek. *Giving a "Square-Toed Packet" a tow, the sturdy little steam-tug* Amalie *brings in a scow schooner heavily laden with a cargo of bricks, on an afternoon when the wind has disappeared and the channel water is as still as glass.*

The Busiest Part of the Waterfront. *Mission Creek was a narrow canal for so much activity. Captain Fred Klebingat recalled: "In 1909, when I was donkeyman on the* Annie E. Smale *we were discharging at Pope & Talbot's wharves, at the entrance to Channel Creek. The hay wharves were just opposite. I was sitting in my cabin one day when lo and behold here comes the end of a bowsprit right through the porthole! There was some muffled shouting; I could hear the flapping of sails, and the next thing I knew the bowsprit backed out and was gone. It was a scow schooner, temporarily out of control. No harm done."*

1906 Earthquake Hits Mission Creek and Butchertown

The spectacular sight of downtown San Francisco burning attracted everyone with a camera and film during those perilous days in April 1906. South Beach escaped the fire by a few blocks. The Oriental Warehouse at First and King was untouched, and earthquake damage in the Mission was not spectacular enough to compete with the smoking ruins of the demolished city. However, in a row of Victorian houses, several collapsed on their foundations while others did not. Their angle of repose was dramatic enough to catch at least one photographer's eye. According to the penned note under the picture in Roy Graves' scrapbook at the Bancroft Library, these houses were undermined because they were built over the subterranean waters of Mission Creek. The address is given as Howard Street, and the house on the right is number 2119. An 1869 Coast Survey Map laid over the 1906 street map shows a wide curve of Mission Creek formerly on this site; by 1884 the area had been filled-in and built upon.

The great fires that burned the city started from broken gas mains, but lack of pressure from broken water pipes left the fire fighters with no means of control, so they faced the painful last resort of dynamiting buildings in the path of the fire. Failure of the water supply prompted a post-earthquake investigation in 1908 from which the city engineers and officials of the Spring Valley Water Company reached these conclusions:

Undermined By Mission Creek. *The flats at 2119 Howard and the adjoining house sank both backwards and sideways. For more than twenty years Mission Creek lay sealed-in, directly beneath.*

"With few exceptions these [water main] breaks may be segregated into several well defined groups which are located on areas of soft alluvium and in artificially or *made ground* and failures occurred in practically all such areas in which there were pipe lines. Investigation of the causes of the breaks located in apparently firm ground shows that the majority of those in the burned district were caused by the use of dynamite, by impact due to the fall of heavy portions of buildings on the streets directly over the pipes or by explosions of nearby gas mains . . .

"From this investigation the following conclusions have been reached:— First—the destructive effects of earthquakes in the City will be far greater in areas of soft alluvium and artificially filled or *made* ground, than on higher firm rocky ground . . . A review of studies made of other great earthquakes shows that investigators have generally found that the destructive effects were similar to those resulting from the California earthquake of April 18, 1906, namely, other things being equal, structures situated on firm rocky ground with the exception of those over or near a fault plane along which movement occurred, suffered comparatively little damage and the serious effects were generally confined to areas of soft alluvium or artificially filled or *made ground*." (Italics as published.) Their conclusions are followed by notes from geologists and engineers regarding earthquakes studied from Port Royal, Jamaica, in 1692, forward to the Andalusian earthquake of 1884—all cite the problems experienced with structures built on marshy or man-made ground.

The report went on to make various recommendations for auxiliary water supplies to avoid future uncontrolled burning in the city. They made the following cautionary statement: "Buildings on areas of artificially filled land or *made ground* are to be afforded the same protection as those situated on more solid ground, but the probability of the entire fire protection system of the city being put out of service by the destruction of fire mains in these areas is to be guarded by special arrangements of pipe and gate systems."

Accompanying this investigative report is a map showing locations in the city

Butchertown Collapses. *First Street, on the marsh of Islais Creek, the street that the butchers had piled and capped in the mid-1870s, collapsed, dumping wooden structures into the bay. The man in overalls, standing astride the two planks with his arms folded across his chest, is John James White—he recycled the sagging saloon front into a new home on Berlin Street. Workingmen on the Potrero were thrifty—everything was salvaged and put to use. Rebuilding San Francisco turned their economic lives around—at last everybody had a job they could count on.*

where water mains of the Spring Valley Company were broken. The old Willows resort built in the 1850s flooded out in 1861; again this trouble-plagued site shows an alarming concentration of broken pipes between Eighteenth and Nineteenth streets. Here had been the fresh-water lagoon where the founders of the mission pitched their tents in 1776 and waited for word of the *San Carlos*. Further damage occurred on Harrison and Bryant—generally following buried Mission Creek's meanders through the vanished saltmarsh.

Of more than passing interest is the 1906 photograph of the collapse of Butchertown at Islais Creek. This is a rare view of a relatively insignificant place about to slide into the bay. Its importance lies in the fact that the Islais Creek drainage is the southern twin of Mission Creek and Mission Bay.

The persistence of such geographic features as underground streams and filled-in coves and bays is of great importance to city planners in San Francisco. An air view of the Mexico City earthquake of September 19, 1985, revealed that the worst damage to the city occurred within the outline of the ancient dry lake underlying Mexico City.

Ted White Recalls—"The morning of the earthquake I was living in Butchertown at 1574 Seventh Avenue (now Galvez). The thing that I remembered in the earthquake was 'Bang! Bang! Bang!' It shook—really badly—and all of a sudden the brick chimney, a short red brick chimney, disintegrated and the bricks dropped down. You see, in the picture, my father with his arms crossed and the other guys. There was a saloon that collapsed in those buildings and because of the instability of the foundation, this saloon went right down into the water and was floating away. A couple of fellows and my father went to the guy that owned it and said, 'Well, what are you going to do with your saloon?' And the fellow didn't know what to do. 'Cheez, I got $50, or $200, or maybe $300 worth of booze in the joint and I don't know what's going to happen now.' My father says, 'I'll tell you what we'll do. We'll buy it.' So two fellows, maybe three, bought it. They towed the thing over to the Hawaiian Fertilizer Company and pulled it up on part of the beach so that they could get to it. The lumber was hauled to Berlin Street and our father built our house out of the saloon lumber from the earthquake. . . ."[114]

William Kortum Remembers—If there was one effect of the earthquake for San Francisco's working class, it was to put everyone back to work for a substantial period of time. The building trades boomed and, on Channel Street, young William Kortum from Calistoga was at work in the E.K. Wood lumberyard. Kortum hoped to work in the yard rather than clerk in the office: "But scarcely a day did I spend at that occupation, for orders and teams came in by the hundreds and now I am at my old work again, only very much busier than formerly . . . As my work is much harder than before the fire I shall demand more pay in the future and as soon as things get settled, apply for work in the yard again.

"On *one* morning we sell more lumber than in a week before the fire, and all the lumber firms must be getting rich. Of course payment is doubtful and all trade is a matter of lottery at present, but they seem to feel confident of getting their pay.

"I am now sitting on a high lumber pile, in the warmth of the mid-day sun, just opposite to our yard office, the busiest place south of the channel, except for the Union Iron Works. Below me, dozens of teamsters are impatiently waiting for one o'clock to get their loads, while the tired and over-worked tallymen and yard-hands, their dinner over, are lying outstretched on piles or lounging in doorways. Some of the teams of horses have stood here for several hours, and as many more may pass away before they leave with their goods.

"Lumber dealers estimate the quantity of lumber needed to rebuild San Francisco as it formerly stood at three billion feet."[115]

LIVING MEMORIES, 1931-1960

The fleet of steam schooners moving along Channel Street served the booming lumberyards during reconstruction after the earthquake. These flush times gradually changed to the lean times more customarily associated with the working class and the waterfront. There was a big (but temporary) blip of prosperity brought on by the need for ships during World War I, but by the '20s hard times were back.

After the stock-market crash of '29, the normally large population of transient, out-of-work men in the south-of-Market area was swelled by waves upon waves of men and boys on the move. One of the boys, Harlan Soeten, arrived in San Francisco at the age of 16 in 1931, hoping to ship out, fascinated by all he had read of life at sea and all he had seen as a young boy hanging around ships at southern California wharves.[116]

Harlan remembers staying first at the YMCA and then at the Coastline Hotel at Third and Townsend, directly across from the railway depot. "The Coastline was a two-story brick building with a cigar store on the corner and the hotel sort of wrapped around it, with shops downstairs and rooms for rent upstairs. There were a number of longshoremen staying there and railroad men who worked across the street. There were two men who loaded the banana boats for the United Fruit Company, down on Mission Creek. At the Coastline we had a community kitchen and pantry where each man could keep his can of beans and bread. The men sat around playing Pedro, an interesting card game that I never heard of, before or since.

"Then my money ran out and the next thing I remember I was in a real flop house, the Standard Hotel on the corner of Seventh and Harrison. It was a larger, two-story hotel with a sort of entry space guarded by a man who pushed a button to let you in or out. The lobby was a big, dark room with benches and tables. At night they would string up clothesline over the benches and you could rent space for 10 cents a night to sleep, sitting on a bench with your elbows

Channel Street From the Air in 1923. *Railroad freight cars are lined up waiting for the banana boats in an era still dominated by railroad transportation for freight. Beyond the China Basin Building are the Southern Pacific freight warehouses to the left and the covered platforms for thousands of rail commuters from the peninsula. The Mission Revival depot at Third and Townsend appears on the far right.*

RUSSEL AERO FOTO, CHS

hooked over the rope. Rooms were 25 cents but I wound up in the dormitory, a big downstairs room in back of the washroom. The city rented this space for soup kitchen workers who got free lodging, two meals a day and a package of Bull Durham Tobacco once a week. You bought your package of cigarette papers for a nickel.

"I was picked out of the line by the deputy sheriff who ran the soup kitchen for the city on Clara Alley, near Howard. We served oatmeal in the morning and there would be a line of men, five and six abreast, filling up the alley and extending around to Howard. We'd set up oatmeal, slice bread, and serve coffee and prunes. At 3 o'clock we'd serve hot stew. Those were the two hot meals a day. And the sheriff had a counter to keep track of how many we fed. As I remember, it was 4,000 men at each meal. Of course there were many other soup kitchens—I remember using six different ones.

"I remember walking down to Mission Creek in 1931 and '32. The United Fruit boats couldn't turn around in the narrow channel, so a tugboat would tow the big banana boats in by the bow and out by the stern. These were the famous banana boats that unloaded with conveyor belts into box cars at the China Basin Building. They would have shape-ups there in the early morning, if a ship was due on the pier. There would be crowds of longshoremen waiting, hoping for work. The star-gangs were paid by the company and they got the first chance at being hired. If they needed more men the walking boss hired the extra men. He'd say, 'That's all,' and they would drift off looking for work somewhere else. If a banana boat was due in at 10am and got held up by fog until noon, nobody got paid until noon. There was a lot of standing around and hoping, down on Channel Street and all along the waterfront in the '30s."

To have a chance at even one of the 3,000 jobs controlled by Terry Lecrouix, the Dollar Line shipping master, Harlan had to get a shipping card at the "fink hall," run by the Waterfront Employers Association, and a discharge card from another ship. Only as a work-away could he get that important discharge card. The work-away was paid one dollar a trip, on the theory that he was a stranded sailor trying to get to the next port and willing to work his way there. It was a pool of free labor that kept a lot of men out of work.

The Strike—In 1933, paybacks, graft, bribery and plummeting pay—the average weekly wage earned by star-gang longshoremen dropped to $10.46—produced a situation ripe for union action. That same year the National Recovery Act recognized the right of American workers to organize and bargain collectively. In February 1934 the International Longshoremen Association met in San Francisco and made demands on West Coast shippers. They wanted a minimum of $1 an hour and $1.50 overtime, a six hour day and, most important, the elimination of the shape-up system of company hiring. The strike set for March 7 was moved forward to May 7. All up and down the West Coast other maritime unions joined, and thousands of men didn't turn up for work.

San Francisco's *Examiner* campaigned to break the strike and on July 5, 1934, thousands of pickets tangled with strikebreakers and police on what was to be remembered as "Bloody Thursday." Strikers and sightseers were driven up the reaches of Rincon Hill by police throwing tear gas. Royce Brier of the *San Francisco Chronicle* wrote this eloquent description: "Blood ran in the streets of San Francisco yesterday. In the darkest day this city has known since April 18, 1906, one thousand embattled police held at bay five thousand longshoremen and their sympathizers in a sweeping front, south of Market Street and east of Second. Two were dead, one was dying, 32 others were shot and more than three score sent to hospitals."[117]

On July 16 a general strike of sympathy involved every union worker in San Francisco and Alameda counties. Two thousand National Guardsmen patrolled the waterfront, some in small tanks. Reluctantly, the Waterfront Employers

Association submitted to federal arbitration and Harry Bridges sent his workers back to work on July 31st. Two months later union hiring halls were a reality.

But the depression remained a fact of life. Until 1941, and our entry into the Second World War, jobs were few and far between on Channel Street and for the workers of the Potrero and Mission Bay.

Longshoreman Al Ohta Recalls:—"From 1947 through 1959 there were too many longshoremen for the number of jobs available so the books were closed. Finally in 1959 a large group of us, between 600 and 800, were added to the books. There were "A" men and "B" men, and the B men got the Mission Creek banana boats because it was dirty, strenuous work.

"The green bananas were stowed in the hatches on their stalks. There were two groups of workers. One fed the banana stalks onto the conveyor belt that brought the fruit up out of the hatch. The dock group walked the bananas from the belt to the chilled refrigerator cars on the siding next to the China Basin Building. There was never much room between stalks so nobody wanted to work on the end of the conveyor belt where the bananas would fall off.

"Every few hours we would shift cars and everybody looked forward to that break. It took nine hours to complete a ship. It only paid $2.85 an hour in 1959. You depended on extended hours, and overtime made us well-paid workers. We got time and a half after six, not eight hours.

"The banana boats were known to be more boisterous, with more drinking going on. There was a lot of good feeling and humor and a big crap game going on that really upset the wives so much the company put a stop to it. Many of the longshoremen worked partners. Some men had the same partner on jobs for years. If a man died he might leave his property to his work partner rather than his family. Speaking of dying, you had to die on the job to collect union benefits and there is a story of a longshoreman dying at Crabby John's (Blanche's today) and his buddies stowed him in a box car so his widow would collect.

"The key to Bridges' success was the honor system in the hiring hall. You get there early, about 6:30 a.m., and you have rotary hiring with the fellows with the least hours that month getting the first jobs. Start fresh every month. This system zeroed in on the problem of how to make the work fair. Bridges was a very creative guy. He got all for the men that he could out of the transition from bulk cargo to container ships."[118]

Battle of Rincon Hill. Waterfront strikers joined by union members from all over the bay area and the Pacific Coast lined the upper reaches of what was left of Rincon Hill. As tanks rumbled down the Embarcadero, tear-gas kept the strikers back. It was a dark day in San Francisco and, for San Francisco's merchant marine, the beginning of the end.

SIXTY-TWO

LIVING MEMORIES, 1959-1986

"It is a living community. New people appear and the creek trains them to live upon it. There is literally no room to slip up. The dock is narrow and the channel's inward and outward currents are sometimes unforgiving. Other times, it's a piece of cake on a glassy lake—a laid-back dream . . . It's an acquired taste to stick with an inlet that takes your house up six feet and then down six feet, twice in every twenty-four hours . . . that absorbs the effluvia of storm drains and simulates a sewer, and then two days later wins your heart back with a blue-lake duck . . ." Sharon Skolnick, houseboat resident on the Channel.

On the last remaining sliver of water marking all that is left of Mission Creek and historic Mission Bay, a miniscule fleet of twenty houseboats lies at permanent moorings, sharing the harbor with thirty-five fishing boats and a gathering of watercraft that carry on a San Francisco tradition dating back to rowing and yachting clubs founded on Long Bridge in the 1860s. The 1973 aerial view at left shows the giant stub of freeway nearing completion at its break-off point.

The scope of the technologies invented in the last twenty years is matched by the extent of the bureaucracies that manage them. "If you don't exist on paper in an E.I.R., then you just don't exist at all," the survey lady said cheerfully to the harbor community, who are somehow not convinced that paper has a more essential reality than people. Again and again the little community has been kicked by the unthinking foot of authority that could sink them all unless they resisted.

In 1960 the state of California moved the houseboat and boaters community out of Islais Creek Basin and gave them fifty-five permanent berths on Channel Street. Ruth Huffaker remembers the channel in 1959 when she and her husband, Steve, kept their cabin cruiser there; they built their first houseboat in 1962. "This was just like country then. We had jack rabbits and foxes. I only saw the foxes at night when their eyes flashed green in the headlight beams. The street was all cobbles.[119] In the winter you had to drive all the way around because the street became a lake. There was an old fig tree and a beautiful old deserted house, completely surrounded by six-foot weeds—probably fennel and dill. There were tomatoes from some lost garden out there, and wild blackberries.

"The weeds were so tall that men made little homes in them. You never saw them; they ran if they heard you coming. You'd hear a little rustle and they would be gone. It never bothered me to walk out there. I felt safe at 2 a.m. It was the country in the middle of the city and the bums made it their own. They didn't bother us and we didn't bother them. They drifted off in the '60s because the truckers and wholesalers commercialized the place on either side of the channel. Cut down the weeds. But before, in the summertime, you couldn't see anyone walking through. You'd just discover things, like a hole in the ground with rocks around to cook on. One place had two mattresses and a coffee table. It was fascinating to me."[120]

Ruth remembers building her first houseboat on weekends and vacations; she was in electronics and her late husband, Steve, was a welder. "Built our first houseboat in '62 and four years ago we built this one. But it was the people in the harbor who really built this boat. I mean, we have carpenters and electricians down here. Everybody helped. Keith Oakford did the complete inside and didn't charge us a dime. Isn't that wonderful? Everybody loves Keith. This ramp will stick up in the air and I will get on the phone and say, 'Keith, the ramp is stuck.' He comes on over and the next time I look, it's fixed."

In 1969, when the Burton Act transferred the port from the state to the city,

Freeway Nears Completion to Nowhere. *A 1973 aerial view demonstrates the fragile life of the houseboat and boat community. The Fourth Street bridge crosses the waterway at the top of the view, reaching Blanche's small seafood place on the water—perhaps the oldest waterfront cafe in San Francisco. The south side of Channel Street is dominated by low warehouses and trucks. Pilings on the north side of the creek serve as perches for egrets and herons fishing for smelt.*

a grandfather clause required that the city provide the houseboat community with comparable berths if the occupants were forced to move. Since the amenities of Channel Street are unique, the clause seemed to guarantee a safe haven. But although this is the law, various agencies had to be reminded of its existence.

Ruth had lived on the channel for thirteen years in 1974 when Sharon Skolnick moved into the *Azteca*, a truncated, wooden-pyramid of a houseboat. Ruth remembers that there had been a fire in the sheds up on the opposite bank and their electricity had been cut off. "The very next day there were reporters around where the pier had been burned and I had to keep telling them to watch their step. A strange man came down and I said, 'What are you here for?' And he said, 'Well, I'm from the Port, and Monday morning I'm supposed to tear this thing down. The whole thing, and put the boats in locked storage." Sharon recalls: "The next day all the boats had eviction notices stapled on them: 'You are hereby notified that on Monday (as of the previous month) you are evicted.' My boss, Rose Farrington, called a TV station to say, 'I'm a concerned citizen and I hear that they are going to evict the people on Mission Creek and I think it's an outrage. Could you cover it?' They were typically noncommittal, so she called another station and said, 'Well, Channel 5 said they were going to go down and see what was up.' "

Meanwhile, Ruth called the newspapers and the TV newsmen as well. "I called Channel 7 and they didn't know anything about it, so I said, 'Well, I have to hang up, Channel 4's camera just came down on the float outside.' They decided to come right out." Sharon's television interview got across the idea that "this isn't just another place to live, this is a real community. The coverage was so sympathetic that the port must have been embarrassed. They put the eviction notice on hold and they wound up building us a new float." So in 1974 Channel Creek houseboaters won another battle to exist. The *San Francisco Progress* ran a headline: "Ruth Huffaker says, 'It's true, you can beat City Hall!' "

In July 1976 an agreement was reached among the boat owners, the San Francisco Port, Bay Conservation and Development Commission, and the Army Corps of Engineers. A lease was negotiated, the port removed the old piers and built new berths from salvaged material at a cost of about $170,000. The Mission Creek Harbor Association was formed and, in November 1977, they took on the management of the Channel Street harbor.

Ruth's houseboat has been the association's frequent meeting place and she confessed, "I've never made such good friends in my life as I have on the Channel. Everybody is so close. They help each other. It's really fantastic. There is so little sense of neighborhood in the city and no sense of community to compare with this. We have work parties to clean up the wharf. Cook hamburgers and hotdogs on the grill up there. People make salads to feed the people who are working. And it is a reasonable place to live in the city where nothing else is. The harbor is a finite thing. We are limited to just twenty houseboat berths and thirty-five others. We pay property tax now like everybody else and I would rather be legal than have to keep looking over my shoulder to see who is coming to throw us out. I've chaired a lot of meetings fighting for this harbor. One thing that binds houseboat people together is fighting for our right to survive. Whatever our differences are, when we have such a common need it brings us close together.

"We have all this wildlife around here. We share our boats with the birds. White egrets have had babies down here. Elusive night herons nest nearby. Harbor seals come in—not often, but it's fun when they do. Anchovies come in and at night their scales flash with a kind of silver phosphorescence. There's always something alive out there. Two years ago it was jack rabbits and we fed them scraps to keep them from eating our community garden.

"Actually, this is the world. As small as we are, we represent a real cross-section

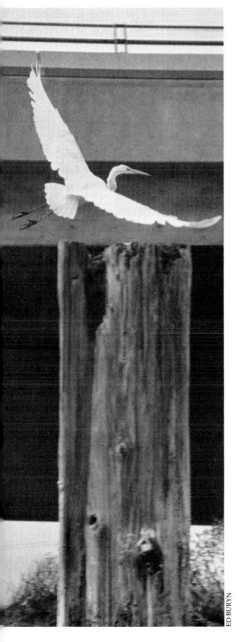

Egret versus Freeway. The paradox of this century is the persistence of these fragile birds in an increasingly inhuman environment.

ED BURYN

ED BURYN

of America in these few boats. A couple of doctors live here, engineers, carpenters, writers and artists. Some retired people. It's such a shame that retirees have to wind up living in flimsy trailers on paved parking lots when they could live like this.

"I've been on the waterways everywhere in the United States and no matter where I go, I always find a little houseboat community trying to exist, just to enjoy living so close to natural things. As they get older, it is so important for people to be connected to the natural world. Even though it's hard to always have to deal with the elements. Still I enjoy sitting here in the morning over my cup of coffee, watching the birds preening on the pilings over there, looking at the smelt running and watching a pelican making a dive for them. Something different is happening out there all the time. Not a single weekend passes that couples don't come knocking on my door and plead with me to find them a berth so they can live on a houseboat, too. But there are only twenty and that's all there are. I hate to tell them that. You'd think with all the waterways around San Francisco Bay there would be enough room to give people a place to live that they could enjoy as much as we do."[121]

Eye-level View of the Harbor Community. *Mostly built by hand, these modest floating houses are home to a wide variety of San Francisco professionals, artists and writers, retired people and office workers. Living close to the water under the shadow of the freeway, their important connection to a natural world is the wildlife of the waterway.*

NOTES

1. San Francisco's rowing clubs used the sunny expanse of Mission Bay and Long Bridge from the 1860s right up through the turn of the century. The clubhouses of the Ariel and South End rowing clubs were moved to Aquatic Park in San Francisco in the 1930s.
2. James Roxburgh was the historian for the *South of Market Journal* during the 1920s and '30s. His recollections match the city directory addresses from 1875 through 1880. A man of many south-of-Market trades, he was a frequent toast-master at picnics and banquets, holding forth on the good old days of his boyhood on the south waterfront. Bound copies of a complete run of the *South of Market Journal* may be found in the California History Room of the San Francisco Public Library.
3. George D. Louderback, *Geologic Guidebook of San Francisco Bay Counties*, Bulletin 154 (San Francisco: Division of Mines, 1951), 85. Salem Rice, geologist, comments "When San Francisco's ancient river canyon was cut, 15,000 to 20,000 years ago, the sea level was more than 300 feet below its present level and the coastline was on the far side of the Farallon Islands."
4. "On the average, sea-level in the vicinity of San Francisco Bay rose about 2 cm/yr from 9,500 to 8,000 years ago, but it has risen only 0.1–0.2 cm/yr from 6,000 years go to the present. . . . The rising sea entered the Golden Gate 10,000-11,000 years ago . . . an estuary then spread rapidly, advancing about 30 m/yr along the course of the trunk stream draining the site of southern San Francisco Bay and reaching the vicinity of Menlo Park by 8,000 years ago . . . Most of the bayward growth of marshes has occurred during the past several thousand years as evidenced by lower intertidal and subtidal deposits which typically lie no more than a few meters below mean sea level, beneath historic salt marshes." Brian F. Atwater, Charles W. Hedel, and Edward J. Helley, *Late Quaternary Depositional History, Holocene Sealevel Changes, and Vertical Crustal Movement, Southern San Francisco Bay, California*, Geological Professional Paper 1014 (Washington, D.C.: United States Government Printing Office, 1977), 11-12; Louderback, (from Hoover-Young Bay Bridge Committee Report) 7-8.
5. Michael G. Barbour and Robert Craig, Frank R. Drysdale and Michael Ghiseline, *Coastal Ecology: Bodega Head* (Berkeley: University of California Press, 1973), 157ff.
6. James Roxburg, *South of Market Journal* (October, 1926).
7. H.H. Bancroft, *History of California*, 7 vol. (San Francisco History Company, 1884-1890), vol. 1:293-294, footnote.
8. Roger R. Olmsted and Nancy Olmsted, *Research Design to Locate Nelson Shell Mounds* (San Francisco: San Francisco Clean Water Program, 1981).
9. Richard Levy, "Costanoan," *Handbook of North American Indians* (Washington, D.C.: Smithsonian Institute, 1978), 485.
10. F.W. Beechey spoke of the "Alchone" and the "Olchone" in 1826, placing them as a tribelet living on the seacoast between Monterey and San Francisco. Their harvest of abalone would have been prodigious on this stretch of coast. Levy p.494; Malcolm Margolin, *The Ohlone Way* (Berkeley: Heyday Press, 1978), 34.
11. Fray Francisco Palou *Account of the Founding of San Francisco*, edited by H.E. Bolton (Berkeley: University of California Press, 1930), vol. 3:129.
12. Levy, "Costanoan," 493.
13. G.H. von Langsdorff, *Voyage Down the Bay, 1806*, edited by Joseph Henry Jackson in *The Western Gate* (New York: Farrar, Strauss and Young, 1952), 39.
14. Louis Choris, *Voyage Pittoresque du Monde* (Paris: Firmin Didot, 1822).
15. Theodore H. Hittell, *History of California* (San Francisco: Pacific Press Publishing House & Occidental Publishing Company, 1885), vol. 1:392.
16. H.E. Bolton, *Font's Complete Diary, 1776-1777* (Berkeley: University of California Press, 1933), 259ff.
17. Bancroft, *History of California*, vol. 1:406.
18. Ibid. vol. 1:653.
19. Otto von Kotzebue, *Voyage of Discovery in the South Sea* (London: Longman Hurst, Rees, Orme and Brown, 1821), 132.
20. F.W. Beechey, *Narrative of a Voyage to the Pacific* (London: Henry Colburn & Richard Bentley, 1831), vol. 2:17-20.
21. J.S. Hittell, *History of the City of San Francisco and Incidentally of the State of California* (San Francisco: A.L. Bancroft & Company, 1878), 6-7.
22. von Langsdorff, 38-39.
23. J.S. Hittell, *History of San Francisco*, 70.
24. Robert H. Becker, *Diseños of California Ranchos, Maps of Thirty-Seven Land Grants (1822-1846)*, (San Francisco: Book Club of California, 1964), xxii & xiv.

25. Bancroft, *History of California*, vol. 3:698.
26. Rev. Walter Colton, *Three Years in California* (Stanford: Stanford University Press, 1949), 222-223.
27. Rare documents, Spanish-Mexican legal documents, Bancroft Library; William Heath Davis, *Sixty Years in California, 1831-1839* (San Francisco: A.J. Leary, 1889), 199-200.
28. Francisco de Haro bought the *Rancho Laguna de la Merced* from Antonio Galindo for 100 cows and 25 dollars in goods. Galindo's grant had been first made on the San Francisco peninsula. The de Haro claim that made its way through the United States courts until 1868 was for the Potrero lands granted to the de Haro twin boys in 1834. William Crittenden Sharpsteen, "Vanished Waters of Southeastern San Francisco," *California Historical Quarterly*, vol. 21:120.
29. Antonio Berreyesa Recollection, dictated to Don Emillo Piña, translated by Thomas Savage for H.H. Bancroft, Bancroft Library.
30. Theodore Hittell, *History of California*, vol. 1:464-465.
31. Bancroft, *History of California*, vol. 5:563-564.
32. The first sale took place on July 20, 1847; 250 water lots in Yerba Buena Cove were sold at prices from $50 to $600, mostly at or near the higher figure. "The lots between Clay and Sacramento, reserved for possible use by the government, were sold six and a half years later, and brought $12,000 each, on an average—more than one hundred times as much as in 1847." J.S. Hittell, *History of San Francisco* . . . 114.
33. Rev. Walter Colton, *My Three Years in California*, 216.
34. Ibid. 146
35. J.S. Hittell, *History of San Francisco* . . . 153.
36. Ibid. 433-434.
37. H.H. Bancroft observed, "The city's encroachment on the bay created an international sisterhood: Thus were overcome difficulties not unlike those encountered in placing St. Petersburg upon her delta, Amsterdam upon her marshes and Venice upon her island cluster. During the winter 1850-51, over 1,000 people dwelt upon the water in buildings resting on piles and in the hulks of vessels." *History of California*, vol. 4:169.
38. No ordinary men, Frank Soulé, John H. Gihon, M.D., and James Nisbet had, at one time or another, published or edited the *Alta California* (San Francisco's most informative and long-lived Gold Rush newspaper), San Francisco's *California Chronicle*, *Picayune*, and *Bulletin*. The *Annals of San Francisco* covers every important event in the city's history (that appeared in the local press) from 1848 through 1854. Going beyond mere chronology, the annalists attempted to give meaning to the city's astonishing growth from a village to a city in less than a decade.
39. Frank Soulé, John H. Gihon, M.D., and James Nisbet, *The Annals of San Francisco* (New York: D. Appleton & Company, 1854), 215-216.
40. Ibid. 250.
41. Bayard Taylor, *El Dorado, Or Adventures in the Path of Empire* (New York: 1850), 137-138.
42. Bancroft details a specific case: "A lot on the plaza [Portsmouth] which in 1847 cost $16 sold in 1849 for $6,000 and at the end of the year for $45,000." Bancroft, *History of California*, vol. 5:192.
43. Soulé et al, *The Annals of San Francisco*, 372-373.
44. Louis J. Rasmussen, *San Francisco Ship Passenger Lists*, vol. 2:134; Le Count & Strong, *San Francisco City Directory*, 1854.
45. H.B. Tichenor, Recollections for H.H. Bancroft, unpublished ms. Bancroft Library.
46. Citations in this section refer to early Deed Books (1848-1854) in the archives of the City of San Francisco, Recorder's Office. Deed Book 4:595-596; Deed Book 27:560.
47. Deed Book 27:573 and 595.
48. Deed Book 45:308.
49. Deed Book 20:536.
50. William S. Jewett, portrait painter, letters. Bancroft Library.
51. *Dictionary of American Biography* (New York: Scribner, 1933), vol. 10:73. John McHenry is listed as Judge McHenry in society columns of the 1850s but he continues to be shown as an attorney in the city directories up through 1868. He shared Jewett's southern sympathies as he was arrested for "enticing a private on Alcatraz Island to join an anti-Union activity" in 1861. After 1880 he is no longer listed in San Francisco city directories.
52. Theodore Hittell, *History of California*, vol. 1:226.
53. Bancroft, *History of California*, vol. 4:576.
54. Theodore Hittell, *History of California*, vol. 2:754.
55. J.S. Hittell, *The History of the City of San Francisco* . . . 181-182.
56. U.S. Patent Book #204797, Plat of Pueblo Lands of San Francisco, December, 1883. F. Von Leight, U.S. Deputy Surveyor, Ms. in Archives of the City of San Francisco, Recorder's Office.
57. H.H. Bancroft, *History of California*, vol. 4:576-577.
58. Ibid. 577.
59. Jasper O'Farrell's letters concerning surveys and property in the San Francisco area. Ms. at California Historical Society.
60. "Census of the inhabitants of both sexes in the jurisdiction of San Francisco for the year 1842." Original signed by Francisco Sanchez, 1842. Typescript ms. at California Historical Society. Francisco de Haro's wife, Emiliana, was the daughter of Jose Sanchez, owner of the *Rancho Buri Buri*, located south of C. Bernal's rancho in south San Francisco. "California Rancho Under Three Flags," *California Historical Quarterly*, vol. 17. No. 3 (September, 1938), 255.
61. *California Statutes* (May 10, 1854), Chapter XXXIX, Sections 1 & 2:44.
62. Bancroft. *History of California*, vol. 3:187ff.
63. Davis, *My Sixty Years in California*, 315.
64. *San Francisco Chronicle*, August 18, 1878.
65. *California Statutes*, 1854, pp. 18-19; 1855, pp. 270-271.
66. *South of Market Journal* (October, 1923), 24.
67. *San Francisco Municipal Reports*, 1870-1871, 508.
68. Lamott and Gihon, attorneys' letters at California Historical Society.
69. Soulé et al, *The Annals of San Francisco*, 663.n
70. Ibid. 664.
71. Charles Lockwood, quoting a letter by Hinton R. Helper in *Suddenly San Francisco* (San Francisco: San Francisco Examiner, 1978), 126.
72. Soulé et al, *The Annals of San Francisco*, 160-161.
73. North, E.M. "Evolution of Shipping and Shipbuilding in California." *Overland Monthly*, February, 1880: 143-153.
74. Roger R. and Nancy Olmsted, *San Francisco Waterfront* (San Francisco: San Francisco Clean Water Program, 1976), 167-168.
75. Soulé et al, *The Annals of San Francisco*, 160.

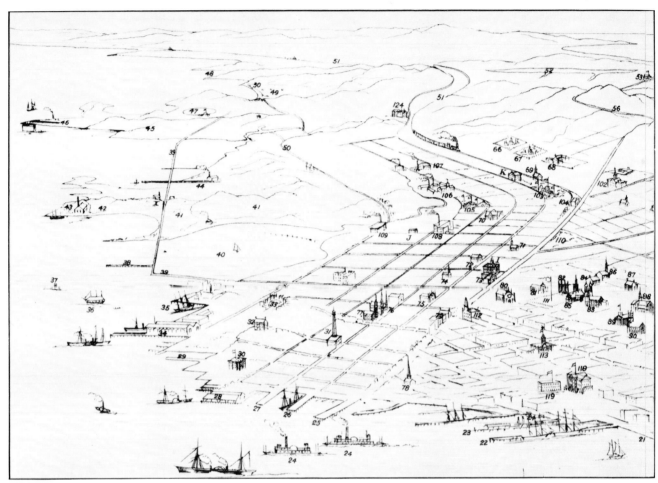

76. Key to Gray & Gifford's View of San Francisco, 1869, Mission Bay portion.

25. Market Street Wharf	35. Tichenor's Marine
26. N.A.S.S. [Opposition	Railway
Line Steamers] Mission	36. U.S. Receiving Ship
St. Wharf	37. Mission Rock
27. Howard St. Wharf	38. Hobbs Wharf,
28. California, Oregon &	off Long Bridge
Mexico S.S. Company	39. Long Bridge
Wharf	40. Mission Bay
29. Main Street Lumber	41. Potrero
Wharves	42. Point San Quentin
30. U.S. Marine Hospital,	43. Pacific Rolling Mills
Rincon Point	44. Tubbs Rope Works
31. Selby's Shot Tower	45. South San Francisco
32. Sister of Mercy Hospital	46. Hunters Point Dry Dock
33. South Park	47. Bay View Race Track
34. Pacific Mail Steamship	
Company Dock	

77. *South of Market Journal*, June 1926, p. 15.
78. Asbury Harpending, *The Great Diamond Hoax and Other Stirring Incidents in the Life of Asbury Harpending* (San Francisco: James H. Barry, 1915), 109.
79. J.S. Hittell, *The History of the City of San Francisco . . .* 365 fff.
80. Ibid. 378.
81. Langley's *San Francisco City Directory*, 1870, 169.
82. Harpending, *The Great Diamond Hoax . . .* 147-148.
83. Ibid. 152-155.
84. *California Reports, 1869* vol. 38:189.
85. J.S. Hittell, *The History of the City of San Francisco*, 380.
86. Henry George's prediction about what the railroad

would bring appeared in the *Overland Monthly* in 1868: "The truth is, that the completion of the railroad and the consequent great increase of business and population, will not be a benefit to all of us, but . . . only to a portion. As a general rule . . . those who have, it will make wealthier; for those who have not, it will make it harder to get. . . . Let us not imagine ourselves in a fool's paradise, where golden apples will drop into our mouths. . . ."

87. Bancroft, *History of California*, vol. 4:143-144.
88. Lucius Beebe, *The Central Pacific & Southern Pacific Railroads* (Berkeley: Howell-North, 1963), 19.
89. Mel Scott, *The San Francisco Bay Area* (Berkeley: University of California Press, 1959), 45.
90. The Oakland Waterfront Company stock included 25,000 shares belonging to H.W. Carpentier, 5,000 to John B. Felton and 20,000 shares to Leland Stanford. Bancroft, *History of California*, vol. 4:589.
91. J.S. Hittell, *The History of the City of San Francisco . . .* 374. By now the Central Pacific had bought out all its competition. As governer of California, Leland Stanford had signed several bills, passed by the legislature, favoring his own company. He could do this only in 1862-63, when it was the popular belief that the connecting railroad would be a panacea for all economic woes. Thus federal, county and city subsidies flowed to the railroads in the form of cash and land. "By 1880, the railroads had received patents to 11,458,212 acres. Approximately 16 percent of the entire land area owned by the federal government in California—land which might otherwise

have been open for free settlement—was given to the railroads. As late as 1919, the Southern Pacific Company was still the chief landowner in California.

92. San Francisco, *Daily Evening Bulletin*, June 17, 1870.

93. San Francisco *Call*, October 10, 1872; Carey McWilliams, *California, the Great Exception* (New York: A.A. Wyn, 1949), 95.

94. Bancroft Scraps, *Bulletin*, reprinted from Sacramento *Union*, March, 1868.

95. Ibid. *Bulletin* March 3, 1868.

96. The "Eddy Redline" that appears on various maps of the tideland surveys refers to William Eddy, whose 1849-1850 survey was the first since Jasper O'Farrell's 1847 efforts. In October of 1849 the town council ordered William Eddy to extend O'Farrell's survey, as all the lots had been sold within the old city limits. The Eddy Redline delineates additional lands as far west of the old boundaries as Leavenworth and Eighth streets, near the present Civic Center. By January 1850 more than 3,000 of these lots had been sold.

97. *California Statutes*, March 30, 1868, p.720.

98. In another article on January 10, 1876, the *Bulletin* noted, "Captain John North and Captain Henry Owens had a few sessions earlier applied for 25 year franchises to use the 'mud' and waters ebbing and flowing over it for a considerable distance from the mainland. It was thought proper that shipbuilders of this city should also be entitled to favorable consideration. But these men did not take advantage of the Tidelands Act . . . This exemption [North's and Owen's marine railways] created some dissatisfaction among the fence builders . . ."

99. *San Francisco Bulletin*, January 23, 1877.

100. *Alta California*, August 31, 1878.

101. *Alta California*, August 19, 1878.

102. *Alta California*, January 7, 1872. The same article notes, "The total sales [tideland properties] amounted to $1,477,929.92. With expenses, the State of California netted $1,242,495.92. The University of California was given $200,000 from the sales and a perpetual annuity, according to an amendment of the original Tidelands Act.

103. San Francisco, *Daily Evening Post*, August 1878, and *Chronicle*, November 22, 1889.

104. Sharpsteen, *Vanished Waters of Southeastern San Francisco*," p. 115.

105. Robert O'Brien, "Riptides," *San Francisco Chronicle*, November 22, 1889.

106. State Senator Tom Maloney, "Recollections," *South of Market Journal*, December, 1932.

107. Shipbuilding scraps, National Maritime Museum at San Francisco, p. 129ff.

108. Karl Kortum scraps. Note: Alexander Hay was located at Fifth and Berry, with his launching ways into Mission Creek, and also between Sixth and Seventh, next to Boole's yard. Sanborn Insurance Maps, 1887, Bancroft Library.

109. Captain Fred Klebingat, *Memories of the Audiffred Building & the Old City Front* (San Francisco: Mills Ryland Company in cooperation with the National Maritime Museum, 1983), 14-15.

110. The steam donkey-engine was used on San Francisco docks for lifting heavy cargo. A restored donkey-engine is periodically fired up for demonstration at the Historic Ships' Project in San Francisco.

111. Captain Fred Klebingat, born in Kiel, Germany in 1889, died in Coos Bay, Oregon, in 1985. The last fifteen years of his life were spent in close correspondence and fruitful interviews with Karl Kortum, Chief Curator of the National Maritime Museum at San Francisco, as Klebingat recalled details of his many voyages in square-rigged ships and schooners that sailed every ocean of the world. An omnivorous reader and creative researcher, Klebingat, for example, had annotated R.L. Stevenson's works as he sailed into ports earlier described in these classics. His memory of San Francisco's turn-of-the-century waterfront was specific and honest. Maritime history is far richer for Klebingat as recorded by Karl Kortum.

112. Roger R. Olmsted interview with J. Porter Shaw, March 18, 1951.

113. Marsden Manson, San Francisco City Engineer, *Report on the Auxiliary Water Supply for Fire Protection for San Francisco, California* (San Francisco: Britton & Rey, 1908), 50-55.

114. Ted White interview with Nancy Olmsted, January 6, 1979.

115. William Kortum letter obtained from Karl Kortum.

116. Harlan Soeten interview with Nancy Olmsted, February 13, 1987. Harlan Soeten never got over his fascination with the sea and the ships that sailed. He went on to become curator of San Francisco's Maritime Museum and is now retired—among other things, he recently built a paddle-wheel steamer by hand.

117. Royce Brier, *San Francisco Chronicle*, July 6, 1934.

118. Al Ohta interview with Nancy Olmsted, March 6, 1986.

119. Berry Street, on the north side of the channel, existed as filled land in 1877, from Third Street to the middle of Sixth, as shown on the Index Sheet of the Sanborn Insurance Map for the city. The "cobbles" referred to in this interview are basalt paving blocks. By 1878 three quarters of the city' paving budget of over a million dollars was spent on basalt blocks. They proved to be longer-wearing than the earlier cobblestones, and their flat surfaces were kinder to the hooves of horses and the wheels of vehicles than rounded river-stones. By 1889, under private contract, Fourth Street was paved with basalt blocks from Channel to Kentucky (on the south side of the channel). Most of the basalt paving blocks extant along Channel and Berry today appear to date from the early 1890s.

120. The first account of removing vagrants from this area dates back to 1889, when police descended on the "garbage trust," moved the people out and burned their shanties. From time to time homeless people have sought refuge in this place that has remained remote from city business. On January 24, 1986, history repeated itself as "city officials declared the little village at Berry and Seventh Street to be a health hazard and gave its residents seven days to clear out. In shacks patched together from wood scraps, about two dozen squatters lived in shantytown in a forgotten corner of San Francisco." *San Francisco Chronicle*, January 24, 1986.

121. Ruth Huffaker and Sharon Skolnick interview with Nancy Olmsted, January 26, 1986.

Author's Note & Acknowledgments

My interest in Mission Bay dates back to 1976 when my late husband, Roger Olmsted, and I surveyed the site for possible archaeological finds as San Francisco's Channel Outfalls Consolidation Project got underway. As construction workers dug down near Berry and Seventh Streets they kept finding stoneware bottles of the 1880s that undoubtedly were tossed there by the Boole and Beaton shipbuilders whose picture now appears in this book. Our research and writing about Channel Street eventually appeared in *San Francisco Waterfront* and by 1981, *Bayside San Francisco* explored the larger sites of Mission Bay, the Potrero and Hunters Point.

It was with real pleasure that I undertook to look once again at Mission Bay from the standpoint of social history as well as physical change. Many people helped me. Karl Kortum, founder and Chief Curator of the National Maritime Museum at San Francisco generously shared his collection of notes from Captain Fred Klebingat. David Hull, Chief Librarian of the same institution, gave me intelligent editorial assistance. Lothar Salim was kind enough to give me critical help on the geology of Mission Bay and its relationship to larger San Francisco Bay. Ray Siemers, San Francisco City Hall Historian led me through Deed Books of the 1850s to trace land deals made during the gold rush. Gladys Hansen, City Archivist of San Francisco's Public Library found important photographs that appear, as did Irene Stachura at the Maritime Museum, and the staff of the Bancroft Library and California Historical Society.

Members of Mission Creek Conservancy went over the manuscript with enthusiasm, offering useful suggestions, including recommending people to interview for recent history. I am especially grateful to Cheryl Brandt for her copy editing and technical expertise.

Beyond all these people, the San Francisco Foundation made this book possible with their funding because they felt it was important for San Franciscans to learn about a part of their city that until this day had no published history beyond limited editions put out by San Francisco's Clean Water Project.

Bay View Race Track: Built in 1868 at the end of the Potrero & Bay View Railroad to make the horsecar connection to Hunters Point from San Francisco. Horse drawn streetcars ran out Long Bridge, south from Channel Street, along Fourth and continued south on Third Street. Bay View Playground, between Armstrong and Carrol on Third Street, marks the contemporary site of the long gone ornate pavillion and racetrack.

Butchertown: In the 1850s slaughterhouses were built on the banks of Mission Creek at Ninth and Brannan. By 1869 a city ordinance relocated the butchers south to Islais Creek at First and Kentucky (later known as Railroad Avenue, or Third Street). In both locations tides flushed animal waste into the larger bay.

China Basin: In the 1860s growing trade with the Far East gave rise to exotic names on San Francisco's waterfront: the extant Oriental Warehouse, China Basin, and India Basin. The harbor entrance to Channel Street, extending south to Mission Rock, was shown as China Basin on 1869 maps, a name that persists today. Just south of Mission Rock and north of Potrero Point is Central Basin with India Basin shown as the cove below Islais Creek, lying north of Hunters Point.

Channel Street: As early as 1853 Channel Street was projected in Mission Bay but was not constructed as a protected shipping waterway until the 1870s. The north side was filled in by 1877 with finger piers extending south of Berry Street between Third and Fourth streets. By 1882 the south side of Channel Street from Third to Seventh streets began to be filled. Sometimes called Mission Creek, the channel is the last historic waterway remaining from vanished Mission Bay. Channel Street can be reached by bridges along Third or Fourth Street, south of Berry. It extends inland to Seventh Street.

Hay Wharf: As early as 1876 the hay dealers, who arrived by sail in scow schooners from faraway places like Petaluma, loaded with hay to feed the city's horses, agitated for permission to use the railroad land-grant in Mission Bay to unload and sell their cargo. By 1884 a hay wharf had been constructed on an angle jutting into Channel Street from Pope and Talbott's Lumberyard, between Second and Third, on the north side of the waterway. Nothing remained of the booming hay trade once the truck replaced the horse.

Hunters Point: Shown on 1852 maps as Pt. Avisadero and later as Hunters Point for John Hunter who in the early 1850s failed in his efforts to sell homelots on this isolated peninsula. Cornelio Bernal obtained the original land grant of *Rancho Rincon de las Salinas Potrero Viejo* located in the Islais Creek Basin and Hunters Point. Hunters Point Dry Dock was the first major industry in 1869. Third Street south to Evans Avenue locates today's Hunters Point with its naval shipyard built during World War II.

India Basin: Lies on the north side of Hunters Point, south of Islais Creek. The name appears in the 1860s and persists on contemporary city maps. South Basin is on the south side of Hunters Point and India Basin on the north.

Islais Creek: Derived from the Indian word *islay*, meaning wild cherry, Islais Creek is the southern counterpart of Mission Creek, lying south of Potrero Point and north of Hunters point. Very late in filling, the Islais tidal salt marsh was still being reclaimed in the 1930s. Islais Creek Channel extends from the Army Street Terminal on the north side, east to Freeway 280, and may be crossed on a bascule bridge at Third and Tulare streets.

Irish Hill: From the mid-1870s through 1930, Irish Hill in the Potrero was the center of boarding houses and hotels for men working on Potrero Point in the iron works, refineries and gas works. A serpentine outcrop reached by 98 wooden steps, the hill housed over 800 workmen until World War II when it was leveled. Land east of Illinois Street, from Twentieth to Twenty-Third streets, marks the vanished hill today.

Long Bridge: A causeway to the Potrero, built from 1865 to 1867. Long Bridge started southeast of Berry Street on Fourth Street. The long wooden bridge turned south, following Third Street, crossed Potrero Point and continued through Islais Creek basin to Hunters Point, terminating at the Bay View Racetrack. Built to connect San Francisco to the Potrero and Bay View districts, it had the environmental effect of sealing off the larger western part of Mission Bay, leading to the eventual filling in of the tidal lagoon. No visible trace of Long Bridge exists today, but the contemporary route would be out Fourth to Third, and south to the Bay View Playground at Armstrong and Carroll.

Mission Bay: Appeared on the 1852 U.S. Coast Survey Map, named for the mission founded at the head of the tributary creek. A tidal lagoon of over 500 acres including the extensive salt marshes that reached inland to Folsom and Mission streets, Mission Bay was a wildlife refuge for an immense bird population that fed on its teeming schools of fish, especially the smelt. The 1852 shoreline extended roughly from Third and Townsend, inland to Brannan Street, and west to Seventh and the line of Townsend, crossed the mouth of Mission Creek, and continued in a half-circle to Potrero Point, ending approximately at the modern juncture of Sixteenth and Illinois streets. Only Channel Street remains as a surviving sliver of the waters of vanished Mission Bay.

Mission Creek: A navigable fresh water stream flowing into a tidal estuary, chosen by the Spanish fathers in 1775 as the ideal site for the *Mission San Francisco de Asis*. Springs formed a small falls and pond (located in the modern vicinity of Seventeenth and Nineteenth streets, Valencia and South Van Ness). Today, the juncture of Division and

King streets marks the 1852 site of the tidal entrance of Mission Creek from Mission Bay. By 1874 the creek was vacated as a navigable stream between Ninth and Eighteenth streets. No visible evidence of Mission Creek exists today, although Channel Street is sometimes informally known as Mission Creek.

Mission Dolores: Founded October 9, 1776, by the Spanish fathers Francisco Palou and Benito Cambon. Officially named *Mission San Francisco de Asis*, from very early times it was informally known as the Mission Dolores, referring to Mission Creek's Spanish title, *Arroyo de los Dolores*, named on the last Friday in lent. Dolores in full was *Nuestra Señora de Los Dolores*. Standing today at Sixteenth and Dolores streets, the mission is San Francisco's oldest building.

Mission Plank Road: Opened in the spring of 1851 as a toll road from Third Street to the mission. Built by the Mission Dolores Plank Road Company for $96,000, the franchise allowed owners to collect tolls (50¢ for a horse and cart, $1 for a four-horse team) for seven years. The same company built Folsom toll road in 1853. Both roads set the route for present day Mission and Folsom streets.

Mission Rock: Once a navigational guide for ships, Mission Rock became a dry-dock and warehouse landing for ships. Pier 50 reached out to engulf Mission Rock as the furthest point of landfill of Mission Bay.

Pioneer Race Track: Built in 1850 by A.A. Greene, south of the Mission Dolores, between Twentieth and Twenty-Fourth streets, to take advantage of the springy turf of the marsh. Later sold as homestead lots.

Potrero Point: As late as 1869, official maps named this location Point San Quentin. By 1882, the land projecting from the southern tip of Mission Bay is shown on maps as Potrero Point. Lying to the east side of Illinois Street, and bounded by Twentieth Street on the north and Twenty-Fourth Street on the south, Potrero Point was the center for heavy industry in San Francisco from 1880 through World War I. Among the industries located there: Pacific Rolling Mill, Union Iron Works, Atlas Iron Works, California Sugar Refinery, and the Bethlehem Shipyard.

Rincon Hill: San Francisco's first posh neighborhood extended from First to Third Street , between Bryant and Howard. The 100-foot summit gave residents of the 1850s a view of San Francisco Bay from approximately the same aspect as from the beginning of city's Bay Bridge footing, today. In 1869 the Second Street cut destroyed the hill's integrity and led to its eventual destruction.

South Beach: As opposed to North Beach, referred to a shoreline area (including water lots) south of Rincon Point (Harrison and Spear streets), following an irregular shoreline around Steamboat Point (Second Street past Third, south of Townsend) to Mission Bay. South Beach has been obliterated by landfill.

South Park: Started in 1854 by George Gordon and modeled on an English row townhouse and garden development, this elegant enclave was designed around a central oval park for the residents' use. The oval center, but not the townhouses, still exists between Second and Third, Brannan and Bryant streets.

Steamboat Point: First appeared on the 1852 U.S. Coast Survey Map, southeast of Third and Townsend. A marine railway was shown at Second and Townsend, jutting into the bay. On this narrow stretch of South Beach, John North, Domingo Marcuci, Patrick Tiernan and H.B. Tichenor constructed and repaired the fleet of sternwheelers and sidewheelers that carried gold seekers to Sacramento, and farther. This was the city's prime shipbuilding location from the 1850s through the mid-1860s. Steamboat Point marked the northeastern limit of Mission Bay. Landfill has covered the shoreline of historic Steamboat Point.